It Doesn't
Hurt
Anymore

Release The Past And Embrace Your Future

Elle,

Many Blessings To You

Dr. Arvis Murrell

7/27/19

DR. ARVIS MURRELL

ISBN 978-1-64349-479-1 (paperback)
ISBN 978-1-64349-480-7 (digital)

Christian Faith Publishing, Inc.
832 Park Avenue
Meadville, PA 16335
www.christianfaithpublishing.com

All scriptures, unless otherwise stated, are taken from the King James Version of the Holy Bible

Printed in the United States of America

Dedication

I dedicate this book to my Lord and Savior Jesus Christ. Because of his grace and mercy, I am alive today to tell my story.

Contents

Introduction...7

1 The Woman in the Mirror 9

2 It's All in the Mind..20

3 Facing Adversity...34

4 Wounds of Rejection..47

5 Offense, Resentment, and Bitterness 60

6 Me and My Anger 69

7 The Process of Forgiveness 76

8 When Words Hurt..84

9 How I Escaped the Effects of Alcohol................91

10 When the Vow Breaks 101

11 Grieving the Loss 108

12 Dealing with Depression 115

13 According to Your Faith 128

14 Discovering the Holy Spirit 141

15 Taking Pain into His Presence 150

16 Heart Conditions 162

17 Covered with Guilt and Shame 170

18 From Trauma to Triumph................................178

19 Shaped through Suffering................................189

20 Pain: Part of the Plan......................................199

Introduction
Why the Pain, Lord?

When painful things happen, we often question God. We tell Him we feel picked on and ask how a loving God can allow such hardship. We may even feel like giving up since the pain consumes us. Yet, deep down, we know giving up only compounds the problem.

Just a few years ago, pain gripped my soul. I questioned God about heartaches, losses, and disappointments I had faced. As my emotional wounds began to heal, God reassured me, even on my darkest days, He had not forgotten me. Sometimes He reminded me through Scripture, a message, or simple phone call from a friend. I love how He always provided me with the exact message I needed to keep going.

In the Bible's book of Isaiah, God promises to keep us from drowning in the sea of despair and from burning up by the flames of adversity.

> *"When thou passest through the waters, I will be with thee; and through the rivers, they shall not overflow thee: when thou walkest through the fire, thou shalt not be burned; neither shall the flame kindle upon thee" (Isa. 43:2).*

The Scriptures clearly say when going through deep waters, you will not drown if God is with you. From my experience and from what I have read, you won't even have to try to swim. God parted the Red Sea for Moses and thousands of Israelites. If He did it for Moses, He can do it for you too. God sees the enemy coming up behind you ready to attack, but He does not get upset. He stands ready, with outstretched arms, to bring you your very own Red Sea moment of healing, deliverance, and total restoration if you trust Him.

In this book, I share my personal journey of walking with God and how He has taken my painful past and turned it into His purpose. I wrote this book, first of all, in obedience to God, but I also wrote it to encourage anyone struggling with a hurting heart. Though hard to understand, there's a reason we experience painful events.

God has a purpose for your life. He wants to take your pain under His wings and nurse you back to divine health and wholeness. Then, you can join with me and say, "It doesn't hurt anymore!"

"He sent his word, and healed them, and delivered them from their destructions" (Ps. 107:20).

My Prayer

God can heal in many different ways, including through His word. My prayer is that as you read His word through my message, your heart will be touched, and healing will take place in those areas where you have hurt for such a long time. As God heals you, I ask that you will, in turn, minister comfort and healing to others.

1

The Woman in the Mirror

Remember this popular phrase from the fairy tale movie *Snow White*—"Mirror, mirror, on the wall, who's the fairest of them all?" Although life is nothing like a fairy tale, we should all ask ourselves this question.

When you look in the mirror, who do you see? Do you see someone emotionally scarred from past hurts and disappointments? Or someone harboring deep anger? Maybe you see someone who has been the target of abuse, rejection, and public shame. Or perhaps you are simply not able to see the real you because your fear and pain shadow your lens.

I can still remember the day I stood in front of my bathroom mirror, trying to analyze the woman staring back at me. The woman looked exactly like me, but I did not recognize her. She had the same hairstyle and big brown eyes. She even wore the same outfit. But this woman, broken and scarred, could not possibly be me. However, as I gazed at the reflection, I realized I was this woman who had allowed the painful circumstances of life to dictate her self-worth.

I saw myself as inadequate, incomplete, and not good enough. I simply existed.

As I continued to stare, I began to think about my life and wondered how in the world I ended up like this. I thought about it so hard until I became overwhelmed by a wave of uncontrollable emotions. I had been carrying the wrong mental picture of myself and was not even aware of it.

How did this happen? How did my self-esteem dwindle to nothing? I connected it to painful experiences I'd encountered early in life and the difficult events which occurred later.

Painful and unfortunate circumstances will have a negative impact on how we view things. We end up looking at life through the eyes of pain and can't see what's right in front of us. The pain clouds our vision and leaves us blinded by hurts and disappointments.

A Poor Self-Image

When viewing the world through a scarred soul, everything looks distorted. Painful pasts tarnish our self-images, which simply reveal how we see ourselves and how we judge our worth. A poor self-image causes us to consider everyone else better than ourselves.

My nursing and counseling experience has shown me poor self-image runs rampant in our society today. Young people approach the teenage years believing they don't meet their peers' standards and that they are simply not good enough. They feel inadequate about their appearances, school performances, and relationships. A poor self-image can easily carry on into adulthood, interfering with a person's ability to lead a fulfilling and successful life. A person with a poor self-image thinks she will never amount to anything. She usually accepts poor and inappropriate treatment from family, friends, and even romantic partners.

I remembered going to the fair years ago and visiting a house with lots of mirrors. As I walked inside, these mirrors brought lots of excitement as they distorted my image. I still recall looking at my reflection and seeing an elongated figure in one and a short, wide person in another. All the mirrors twisted my image and didn't represent what I truly looked like. Since I had a poor self-image, this is exactly how I considered myself at times. I saw a person who had been twisted, and my reflection didn't represent me well. I laughed and joked about it at the fair, but the concept is no laughing matter.

Negative thoughts about ourselves contribute to poor self-image, which is exactly what happened to me. I took this distorted view of myself and began to act upon it as if it were true. Although false, once this poor thought pattern developed in my mind, I started to act just like the person I perceived myself to be. I felt like a failure, and then I acted like a failure.

For example, a student who says, "I am dumb when it comes to math," will find her grades to reflect what she says. Do you know why this happens? A person acts out the way she perceives herself.

"For as he thinketh in his heart, so is he…" (Prov. 23:7).

As the above Scripture indicates, we are not the people our mouths declare, rather who we think we are in our hearts. Since our hearts dictate our thoughts, our self-images embedded in our cores manifest themselves in our lives. It's so easy to be caught up in life's painful experiences. Some of us have enough pain to fill novels. But instead of allowing our pains to inflict negative self-images, we need to move toward healing and allow God to give us true reflections of ourselves.

When You Don't Feel Good Enough

I love the movie *Pretty Woman*. I have seen this movie countless times, and each time I look at it, I get a fresh outlook on life. It's like a modern upgrade of *Cinderella*. The story focuses on a young woman living a degraded lifestyle and a rich business man who offers to pay her to be his date at elite business and social functions.

In one of the scenes, Vivian, the lead character, struts into an elegant ladies' boutique on Rodeo Drive in Beverly Hills, California. Instead of being allowed to shop, she gets disrespected and ignored because she does not appear to have the necessary funds for their clothing. Although she had the money, she still leaves the store feeling ashamed and not good enough.

Embarrassed, Vivian goes back to the hotel. Later in the movie, after she has been groomed and coached, she returns.

When the sales associate goes to meet her, she reminds the arrogant clerk of her previous encounter and how she was mistreated. Arms loaded with shopping bags from other high-end boutiques, she tells the sales lady, "Big mistake! Huge!"

For me, it's one of the movie's best moments. I love to see the look on the sale's associate's face as Vivian walks out of the store with all those bags from other businesses. The scene teaches an invaluable lesson. We shouldn't label people who look different from how we think they ought to look. We don't know the plans God has for that person's life and often judge someone before God's transformation takes place.

I compare it to taking a cake out of the oven before it is completely baked. An undercooked cake may appear to be done because the edges are brown. But when we check it, the cake tester doesn't come out clean, because it's mushy in the middle. We don't have to throw the cake away. We can just put it back into the oven and allow it to bake until it is done. Then we'll have a delicious dessert, good enough to eat.

In the same manner, we can't throw ourselves away because we don't like what we see. We also can't allow the opinions of others to stop us. We must respond like Vivian in the movie. If one shop closes the door, go to another store.

We can't allow others to stop us from reaching our goals by dictating how we should look and what we should be doing. Our past doesn't define us. We are just as good as the next person and can do better. Just because we once made poor decisions and lived a less-than-desirable lifestyle, doesn't mean we have to stay in such a position. We can change and be used for a higher purpose.

Why Do I Feel the Way I Do?

To begin my healing journey, I wanted to know why I had such low thoughts and opinions about myself. I began to examine my life by looking into the dark seasons of my soul. After conducting a detailed self-inventory, I identified specific things which had occurred and contributed to my poor self-image.

- *Unstable Home Environment* – A loving and stable home is important for a child's well-being and emotional health. Children need love, acceptance, and attention. I grew up in an unstable home environment due to violence and alcoholism. Yes, I received love, but it came mixed with confusion and fear. Parents with substance abuse issues or other challenges cannot always provide their children with the care, guidance, and attention they need and deserve. This contributed to low self-esteem issues and relationship problems later in my life.

- *Abuse/Trauma* – The abuse and trauma I suffered caused me to feel guilty and ashamed. I even felt I deserved the abuse because I saw myself as unworthy of respect, love, and care. Abuse/trauma left me with a great deal of anxiety, depression, nervous disorder, and overwhelming fear. Naturally, I often felt sad and endured many sleepless nights.

- *Poor Decisions* – Some of the trials and tribulations I endured could have been avoided. I suffered much due to the poor choices I made. Oftentimes, I saw the writing on the wall and received warnings of impending danger around the corner. Instead, I overlooked the caution signs and kept right on going. I guess the temptations were too great. I look back and see where my life could have taken a different path had I made better decisions.

- *Negative Thinking* – I felt and talked about myself in a particular way until it became a habit. My self-image portrayed me as worthless and inferior. I dwelled on negative thoughts, expecting bad things to happen. I rarely envisioned good outcomes, focused on the lack in my life, and believed nothing would ever get better. This negative thinking pattern built a prison in my mind, holding me captive.

My poor self-image was not an accurate reflection of the real me. I realized my low self-esteem and poor self-image reflected the way I felt. I didn't feel good about myself, about what I had done, what I could do, or what I could become. I decided I wanted to make a change for the better, gain a realistic understanding of myself, and discover my worth.

What Does God Think about Us?

There's no better place to begin finding our true images than to start with what God thinks of us. As our creator, He knows who we really are and what we are truly worth. So, to start, I explored the Scriptures for information and was surprised to find God's image of me looked quite different from mine.

> *"And God said, Let us make man in our image, after our likeness: and let them have dominion over the fish of the sea, and over the fowl of the air, and over the cattle, and over all the earth, and over every creeping thing that creepeth upon the earth. So God created man in his own image, in the image of God created he him; male and female created he them" (Gen. 1:26–27).*

> *"And God saw everything that he had made, and, behold, it was very good. And the evening and the morning were the sixth day" (Gen. 1:31).*

According to Scripture, I am made in God's image. Having the "image" of God means God made me to reflect Him and relate to Him through communication and fellowship. God says everything He created was not just good, but very good! This tells me God approved everything. There it is! I bear God's "stamp of approval" because He made me to be like Him, fearfully and wonderfully made.

> *I will praise thee; for I am fearfully and wonderfully made: marvelous are thy works; and that my soul knoweth right well. My substance was not hid from*

thee, when I was made in secret, and curiously wrought in the lowest parts of the earth. Thine eyes did see my substance yet being unperfect; and in thy book all my members were written, which in continuance were fashioned, when as yet there was none of them. (Ps. 139:14–16).

Do you know how wonderful you are? Being wonderful has nothing to do with us, our looks, or abilities. We are wonderful because of who made us. God thought so much of us He took the time and care needed to make each one of us with unique assets.

"For God so loved the world that he gave his only begotten Son, that whosoever believeth in him should not perish, but have everlasting life" (1 John 3:16).

Perhaps you have never seen yourself as important. You may look back on a life filled with pain and disappointment—a deprived and unhappy childhood, a career that never materialized, or years wasted on drugs and alcohol. Your past and future convey the same message. Failure!

Not to Jesus. He loved us so much He gave Himself just for us. God sent His only son to die on the cross for us. Now that's love. I will never ever again think I am not worth anything.

There's More of Me to See

We live in a world where people judge by appearance. We rarely look beyond the physical qualities on the outside such as beauty, talents, fame, etc. To develop a positive self-image, it's imperative we know who we are apart from what we look like and from what we do. If we do not know who we are, we will go through life with very little satisfaction and be disappointed with ourselves.

In my case, I had been working hard on my outer layers yet had failed to identify myself as a person of great value, worth, and made in God's image. I now realize I am more than what you can see. My physical qualities, education, accomplishments, spiritual gifts, and talents do not make me who I am. It is not even my family background, where I live, or what I drive. Even though all these things may be important, they just make up my outward appearance.

If clothes, cars, and material things don't tell us who we are, then who are we apart from all these things? Our true identity plays an important role in determining how we carry ourselves through life, how much peace we experience, how we treat other people, and how we respond to God. It is so easy to be blinded by outer appearances. Even Samuel was swayed by physical appearance.

> *And it came to pass, when they were come, that he looked on Eliab, and said, Surely the LORD's anointed is before him. But the LORD said unto Samuel, Look not on his countenance, or on the height of his stature; because I have refused him: for the LORD seeth not as man seeth; for man looketh on the outward appearance, but the LORD looketh on the heart. (1 Sam. 16:6–7).*

Samuel made the mistake of judging Eliab based on his appearance. Eliab may have looked like a king, but he didn't have the heart a king of God's people needed. It didn't matter how good Eliab looked because God refused him. God does not see as man sees. This passage in the first book of Samuel teaches us a valuable lesson. Our outward appearances do not define us. There is much more of us to see on the inside than the outside. Again, real identity stems from our hearts.

Love Yourself

To most of us, the thought of loving ourselves seems foreign and self-centered. Many of us have such bad self-assessments, we go around carrying trunk loads of bad attitudes, wrong beliefs, and negative self-images. Some of us have been carrying these things for so long that we don't recognize them.

I used to spend a lot of time downgrading myself . . . always beating myself up, seeing myself as not good enough, pushing to be more, do more, just to feel good. I had become completely used up without finding ways to get refilled. Other people and things demanded my attention, so I ended up neglecting myself.

We can't give to others what we do not have. If we don't love ourselves, we have nothing to give. As I looked back over my days, I saw where I always put others before myself, doing as I was taught. While we must think about others, we must also love ourselves before we can truly love our neighbors.

"Honor thy father and thy mother: and, Thou shalt love thy neighbour as thyself" (Matt. 19:19).

Through this Scripture, the Lord tells us it's important to love ourselves as we love other people. He also wants us to love ourselves as He has loved us. Think about it. We can't love others or extend kindness until we let ourselves off the hook.

If you are a person who doesn't think much about yourself, I encourage you to reflect on this message—love yourself. It would be helpful to do a self-check exercise and determine what you think of yourself. It's time to start cultivating a better relationship with yourself, and that means loving who you are. Then you can see yourself as blessed, whole, and healed in Jesus's name.

Learn to Like Yourself

Now that we know how to love ourselves, the next thing is to like ourselves.

While this concept may seem strange, think about how much time you spend with yourself. The fact remains, you can't get away from you even if you try. If you don't like yourself, you are going to be miserable, with no peace.

Our purpose is to live a life pleasing to God. That's illustrated through a life full of love, joy, and having the right attitude toward others and ourselves.

When I struggled with disliking myself, I realized I felt this way because I had talked so badly about myself. I had repeatedly told myself I was too short, too ugly, and I would never make it in life. Talking like this had a negative effect on my confidence and brought sadness. I had to learn to be at peace with my past, knowing it would not stop me from embracing my future. Now I don't have to pretend anymore and put on a front. I can just simply be me because my value and worth stay grounded in who I am in Christ and not dependent upon who I think I am.

> *"For he hath made him to be sin for us, who knew no sin; that we might be made the righteousness of God in him" (2 Cor. 5:21).*

Thanks to the above Scripture, I can be confident in my right-standing with God, only because God is righteous. My righteousness has nothing to do with me, what I have done, or my own striving, but I have been made right through God. This assurance gives me great peace. I have been wrong and errored numerous times. But I am still righteous because Jesus died so I could become virtuous and blameless. Then it makes sense, if God made me righteous, there's no reason to dislike myself, right? The fact is, I never have to feel I'm not good enough, because Jesus makes up for my lack.

You, too, can reverse this pattern by talking positive about yourself. Start praising yourself today, telling yourself you are beautiful, strong, and successful. This doesn't mean you are arrogant. It means you have finally accepted yourself as being created by God, and you are confident in knowing who you are in Him.

When God created us, He gave each of us talents. Instead of focusing on shortcomings, we need to start telling ourselves what we want to do and become in life. Though I have made mistakes, I still like myself. God has given me many gifts and talents to advance His kingdom. When I began changing my thoughts, I went and looked at myself again in the mirror and said, "You are a child of God. You are the head and not the tail. God lives inside of you, and I really do like you."

Because of God's promises and believing in them, I'm no longer confused about my identity. Now I see a confident woman, one who knows where she has been and where she's going.

The Finished Product

While we are busy looking in the mirror at ourselves, Christ creates a new image of us. He works on that picture, and when it is finished, we will be conformed into His image. Christ has already seen the finished work in us. In contrast, we tend to look only at the hurts, pain, anger, wrinkles, hair, and every blemish, but God's work isn't done. The portrait is not finished yet as God's photo lab must put on the finishing touches. Christ works on us every day to get us cleaned, polished, and stamped with His approval in the image of the Son of God.

"For whom he did foreknow, he also did predestinate to be conformed to the image of his Son, that he might be the firstborn among many brethren" (Rom. 8:29).

When you accept Christ, the old person has been transformed into the new person who is like Jesus. Transformation involves a process, so don't be so hard on yourself. Be patient and allow God to continue to do His handiwork in you. He will be working on you until you get to heaven. However, while you are down here on earth, you're continually being changed to reflect the life of Jesus, "the finished product."

2

It's All in the Mind

We can overcome a painful past if we are determined to prevail through life's struggles. But to accomplish this, we need to know where to start making changes and adjustments. Our minds are the control towers for how we behave. If we are serious about turning our lives around and creating lasting changes, the renovations must first start in our minds. Once our minds have made the necessary adjustments, the rest of our lives can follow.

Over the years, I would often convince myself that something was going to go wrong. I just knew I wasn't going to get the job, and then I got the job. I just knew I didn't do well on the test, and then I got an A on the final exam. There were times when I thought every bad headache meant I had a brain tumor, but it turned out to be just a nagging headache. I often look back and wonder why I worried so much and had such a negative outlook. I later realized the problem resided in my head.

An Analytic Mind—The Good, the Bad, and the Ugly

My mind became analytic and curious at a young age. Even before I learned how to read, I would look at the TV and try to figure out how things were made and why people acted the way they did. Once I learned how to read and comprehend in elementary school, I began to read magazines, newspapers, encyclopedias, and anything else that looked worth reading. After high school, I went on to nursing school, then received advanced education in administration and Christian counseling.

As a result of all of this head knowledge, I developed a highly educated mind. Having a mind which is both analytic and highly educated worked for me and against me at the same time.

I have always been fascinated by the human body and how it performs. As a nurse, I quickly became successful at understanding how our bodies functioned normally and how diseases cause our bodies to break down and to not function properly. My analytic mind enabled me to understand complex systems and processes and to gain a position in leadership when I did not have the necessary experience.

On the other side of things, my mind got me into a whole lot of trouble. For example, when I experienced a setback, disappointment, or mental distress, my mind went into overdrive at trying to figure out what and how it happened. Sometimes, I would stay up half the night trying to sort things out by replaying the uncomfortable events and painful memories over and over in my head. The next day at work, I would walk around sipping coffee in an attempt to stay awake. An analytic mind caused me to excel in my career, but it wreaked havoc in other areas. I ended up wasting a lot of time overthinking and reasoning when things didn't make sense. I thought I had to understand everything to walk with the Lord, but God had to show me I did not have to know everything if I trusted Him.

*"Trust in the LORD with all thine heart; and lean
not unto thine own understanding" (Prov. 3:5).*

There have been many times when God left big question marks and empty spaces in my life to stretch my faith. It has been difficult for me to give up reasoning and overanalyzing. But trying to figure out everything exhausted me and took away my peace. So I decided to simply trust God and enter into a place of rest.

Pulling Down Strongholds

The mind is one of the most complicated and powerful parts of the human body, which makes it a key target for the enemy to attack. Satan erects every stronghold he can into our minds to keep us from the true knowledge of God. If he's successful, we cannot enjoy an intimate relationship with the Lord, nor experience His love and awesome power. Overall, if we fall prey to Satan's ploy, we will be emotionally unable to accept God's full affection.

When we have a stronghold in the mind, we've built a spiritual fortress of wrong thoughts. A military term, a fortress is a dwelling place where troops are stationed and operate in power against the enemy. Specifically, demonic forces can hide and operate against us by building a mental stronghold. When we think wrong thoughts, bricks form, and the more wrong thoughts we have, the more bricks stack up. If these bricks are not removed, eventually we will have a tower of wrong thinking built in our minds.

The ideas and thoughts which make up the stronghold are based on lies which challenge the truth about what God has revealed about Himself. Satan's strategy serves to distort our knowledge of God's personality so what we believe ends up being erroneous and inadequate. Thus, we become emotionally weakened and held in spiritual bondage.

Battles have raged in my mind which kept me feeling intimidated, confused, and defeated. I have been plagued with false guilt and tormenting thoughts to remind me of my past failures. Satan has spoken lies in an effort to cripple my walk. He invaded my thought life, causing me to embrace wrong thinking, bad attitudes, and emotional scars.

> *"(For the weapons of our warfare are not carnal, but mighty through God to the pulling down of strong holds;) Casting down imaginations, and every high thing that exalteth itself against the knowledge of God, and bringing into captivity every thought to the obedience of Christ" (2 Cor. 10:4–5).*

In this passage, the apostle Paul tells us we have the weapons we need to overcome Satan's strongholds. When I found out the truth, I understood I could live delivered from unhealthy emotions and be victorious over wrong thinking, which empowered me to partner with the Lord and claim victory.

The key to bringing down mental strongholds lies in knowing God's personality. Getting to know the true God and seeing how He views Christ helped strengthen me on the inside and tear down Satan's lies. The high fortress walls began to fall. Now I can praise the Lord, disarm the enemy, and find life-changing freedom.

A Victim Mentality

Once the strongholds were torn from my mind, one of the first things I found was the Lord wanted to put right thinking into my thought process, which was full of sadness and hopelessness.

You see, I had a victim mentality and viewed myself as a victim and in pain. I pitied myself and thought other people caused my misery. When we blame someone, we make an internal choice in our hearts, leaving ourselves powerless and resentful, which described my mental state. Since life offers challenges, we can easily develop victim mind-sets. As the saying goes, into each life some rain must fall. It's easy to think we've been dealt unfair hands, that while our neighbors bask in sunshine, we're living in never-ending downpours. A person of self-pity says, "You don't know what I'm going through" or "You try living with this twenty-four hours a day and see if you can stay happy."

This may sound strange, but I felt comfortable being a victim. I had grown used to feeling sorry for myself and throwing pity parties.

Being a victim comes in handy when we don't feel like changing. We might blame our troubled childhoods, our alcoholic spouses, or a painful illness. Furthermore, who expects us to move ahead in life? After all we have been through, we have every right to wallow in self-pity.

When we have been hurt, we tend to think of ourselves as helpless beings. But our faith in Jesus makes us more than conquerors through Him who loves us. Nothing, no matter how painful, can separate us from God's love in Christ Jesus.

> *"Nay, in all these things we are more than conquerors through him that loved us" (Rom. 8:37).*

After being paralyzed by pain and self-pity, I discovered God's riches are greater than my problems, and a victory celebration is way more fun than a pity party. I have stopped using my trouble as an excuse. Through allowing myself to accept and receive God's love, I became more than a conqueror.

So can you.

Change Your Thoughts, Change Your Life

Our current culture makes it near impossible to turn on the TV, read a newspaper, go online, or out to eat without our minds being infiltrated by unhealthy thoughts. Our thoughts affect our attitudes and moods. The secret to good mental health remains in knowing which kinds of things to ponder. What we choose to think about and dwell on in life will make us or break us.

I have always been more happy and upbeat when I thought about positive things. But, when I dwelled on the negative side of life, I felt unhappy, pessimistic, depressed, and had a negative attitude. I discovered my thoughts are powerful! All that time, I had cluttered my mind simply by what I thought. If I wanted to change and unclutter my life, I realized it had to begin with my thoughts.

What are you thinking about? Are you constantly thinking about unpaid bills, your troubled relationship, or stressful job? If this is true, according to Paul, you are constantly thinking about the wrong things.

> *"Finally, brethren, whatsoever things are true, whatsoever things are honest, whatsoever things are just, whatsoever things are pure, whatsoever things*

are lovely, whatsoever things are of good report; if there be any virtue, and if there be any praise, think on these things" (Phil. 4:8).

In the book of Philippians, Paul gives us guidelines for thinking. He meant for us to think on righteous things in order to shape our thoughts and behaviors. This Scripture helped me realize I had to be careful about what I paid attention to and where my thoughts dwelled. As I developed a positive mind-set, I chose to think on God's Word, what He says about me and my family, and not think about my circumstances.

Basically, our lives move in the direction of our thoughts. We do not have to become slaves to negative and pessimistic thinking. In other words, we can choose to think about what we want to think about. Our thinking and thought processes do not have to control us, but we can control them. I found out when I resisted and refused to entertain negative thoughts, they left me.

"Submit yourselves therefore to God. Resist the devil, and he will flee from you" (James 4:7).

We are solely responsible for our thoughts, and our outlooks on life are a choice. With practice, positive thinking will help us to take control of our lives and make our everyday experiences more pleasant. Our mental and physical health will also benefit, as it will help us to better adapt to changes and to deal with life's struggles.

Right thinking holds the key to victorious living. Your thoughts are the ever-present currents that move you either closer to or further away from your best future. Think of it from a positive standpoint . . . you are always only one thought away from living the life of your dreams or one decision away from destiny.

Wash by the Word

Do you take a bath every day? That isn't meant to be a physical question but rather it's a spiritual question. We have already established that our minds battle with Satan, who tries to flood our thoughts, desires, and feelings with lies. If we want to win the struggle, our minds have to be washed by the Word. Some of us think like the world, with impure and immoral thoughts.

"And do not be conformed to this world: but be ye transformed by the renewing of your mind, that ye may prove what is that good, and acceptable, and perfect, will of God" (Rom. 12:2).

In order to have a renewed mind, we have to get out of the mud and clean up with spiritual soap and water. Through washing by the Word, our minds are transformed and renewed. Devoting time meditating on the Word of God washes our minds and fixes negative thinking patterns. That's why it's so important to be washed by the Word of God daily.

Through the years, I consumed a huge amount of man's knowledge. While this did wonders for my career, it did little for my spiritual life. When I began to go through the tests and storms of life, I found out screaming and yelling were not effective behaviors for confronting problems. I couldn't cope effectively, because my life was not built upon the Word of God.

One day as I listened to worship music, I heard the Lord speak to me in a clear voice. He said, "You know the word of man, but you do not know My Word." When I heard these comments, I knew exactly what the Lord was talking about. I had too much head knowledge and not enough of His wisdom and revelation. I began to realize I really didn't know God very well. Because God's nature and character reveals itself through His Word, if you do not know His Word, then how can you know God?

"That he might sanctify and cleanse it with the washing of water by the word" (Eph. 5:26).

After this realization, I began to wash my mind by reading just a few verses each day. I read and periodically thought about them. By the end of the day, I had spent an entire day meditating on the Word and usually memorized the Scriptures. I slowly went from reading a few Scriptures to reading chapters. When I started to feel the pressures of life, I was equipped to overcome them with God's Word.

Since prayer unleashes great power when mixed with the anointed Word of God, I even began to pray using the Scriptures. As a result, my mind became saturated with His Word. Gradually, I began turning to Scripture for answers when making decisions rather than trying to think things out for myself. This has enabled me to think differently when trouble comes my way.

Just imagine where you'll be a year from now if you read one chapter and meditate on one specific verse each day. You'll be transformed!

Worrying My Life Away

I grew up believing that worrying made me appear to be a concerned individual. I worried about school grades, family matters, meeting deadlines, bills, appearances, relationships, and anything else possible. In spite of all of my worrying, everything worked out, and I am still alive and well. Instead of wasting time by fretting over things, I could have been living a more positive life. I thought worrying gave me an edge in life, but instead, it kept me on edge. On the verge of a nervous breakdown, I started thinking about my thought life and wondered if God wanted me to worry.

When I conducted my research, I found out worrying was a serious condition which can be dangerous to our health. According to the *Merriam-Webster Dictionary*, worrying is defined as tearing, biting, or snapping, especially at the throat, or to torment with mental distress. This definition gave me greater understanding of worrying's negative aspects, and I began to realize its accuracy. I looked back at my past and identified how worrying had caused me to feel weak and unable to function properly, as if someone had taken me by the throat and cut off my oxygen supply to the brain.

Worrying also serves as a source of torment. When I think of torment, I think of pain and suffering. The Bible speaks of throwing the devil into an unquenchable fire of brimstone, where he will be tormented forever.

> *"And the devil that deceived them was cast into the lake of fire and brimstone, where the beast and the false prophet are, and shall be tormented day and night for ever and ever" (Rev. 20:10).*

In addition to torment, worry attempts to control our destinies, but the Bible tells us we don't have the power to add a single day to our lives.

> *Can all your worries add a single moment to your life? And why worry about your clothing? Look at the lilies of the field and how they grow. They don't work or make their clothing, yet Solomon in all his glory was not dressed as beautifully as they are.*
> *So don't worry about tomorrow, for tomorrow will bring its own worries. Today's trouble is enough for today. (Matt. 6:27–29, 34, NLT).*

Clearly, according to the Scriptures above, worrying wastes time. It won't help solve our problems or make us feel better, and it certainly won't add time to our lives. The enemy wants us to fret over what happened yesterday and worry about what's coming tomorrow. But our God is the God of tomorrows, and nothing in our past has power to define what our tomorrows look like. Because of God's promises, I am learning to live one day at a time and not get ahead of myself.

> *"Don't worry about anything; instead, pray about everything. Tell God what you need, and thank him for all he has done" (Phil. 4:6, NLT).*

In the Bible, Paul tells us to pray about "everything" and not worry. Everything means to pray in every circumstance, good or bad, great or small. Prayer is the perfect remedy for anxiety and worrying. Just think, I could have been praying rather than spending a lot of energy worrying! Now when I pray, I thank God for all He has done for me. Thanksgiving takes my mind off myself and my problems. When I started praying more and giving thanks to God, I had less stress and fewer anxious thoughts.

> *"Look at the birds. They don't plant or harvest or store food in barns, for your heavenly Father feeds them. And aren't you far more valuable to him than they are?" (Matt. 6:26, NLT).*

Have you ever studied birds? I have. They don't have a food store somewhere. In fact, they really are clueless where their next meals will come from. Yet I have never seen a bird frazzled and flipping out over something. God takes care of them. Now aren't we more valuable than a bird? Birds have no control over what happens in their lives and neither do we. We don't have to worry. Things will happen, but God will get us through it. Now instead of worrying, we can spend our lives living.

Thinking through the Storm

When we start out in life, we don't doubt we will make it. But along the way we get distracted, especially when we come upon a big storm. It was easy to trust when the trials were little, but what happens when the situations seem bigger than what we are able to handle? Life's storms can toss us to and fro with winds of grief, fear, and shame. Satan brings storms into our lives to frighten us and to get us to doubt. It can be hard to concentrate. Yet during these times, we need to throw doubt aside and be determined to endure until the end.

When I struggled with doubt, I focused on the storms and felt afraid. I began to think I wasn't going to make it. Concentrating on the wrong things weighed me down physically, emotionally, and spiritually. When going through life's storms, we have to be in the right frame of mind. Peter knew about this all too well.

> *But the ship was now in the midst of the sea, tossed with waves: for the wind was contrary. And in the fourth watch of the night Jesus went unto them, walking on the sea. And when the disciples saw him walking on the sea, they were troubled, saying, it is a spirit; and they cried out for fear. But straightway Jesus spake unto them, saying, be of good cheer; it is I; be not afraid. And Peter answered him and said, Lord, if it be thou, bid me come unto thee on the water. And he said, Come. And when Peter was come down out of the ship, he walked on the water, to go to Jesus. But when he saw the wind boisterous, he was afraid; and beginning to sink, he cried, saying, Lord, save me. And immediately Jesus stretched forth his hand, and caught him, and said unto him, O thou of little faith, wherefore didst thou doubt? And when they were come into the ship, the wind ceased. (Matt. 14:24–32).*

As long as Peter's eyes stayed fixed on Jesus, he was fine. But as soon as he took his eyes off Him, he started to doubt and began to sink. Focusing on what's happening around us causes us to be afraid. We start to think about what will happen next and become fearful. The enemy knows we are defeated if he can distract us with problems, so he tries to get us to take our eyes off Jesus and look at the storm.

What storms of life are you facing right now? Whether it's in your finances, job, family, marital issues, hardship, friends, etc., Jesus promises you victory. Despite trials, you can live an empowered life. Don't allow the storms of life to distract you by looking at the winds and waves. God will be your rescue if you keep your mind on Him. He will establish and launch you into greater things. Stay focused on the Lord, and He will give you strength. Like He did with Peter, He will bring you out of the storm, without a doubt.

Lord, Help My Unbelief

Of all the things which could stop a move of God in our lives, unbelief must be at the top of the list. Doubt does not believe God can do what He says He can do. But unbelief, on the other hand, is a lack of confidence in God. It says we are skeptical about Him and don't trust Him. Jesus encountered unbelief firsthand.

I started out believing God would somehow make a way for me. But as time went by, I thought God had forgotten all about me, because it was taking so long for things to get better. I became angry, felt neglected, and eventually moved into unbelief. I pouted, refused to pray, and failed to go to church. Somehow, I thought I was punishing God. How silly of me!

> *"Jesus said unto him, if thou canst believe, all things are possible to him that believeth. And straightway the father of the child cried out, and said with tears, Lord, I believe; help thou mine unbelief." (Mark 9:23–24).*

"Lord I believe, help my unbelief!" What a confusing statement! The father wanted his child to be healed, but he did not think God could heal him. So, he said, he believed and then wanted help with his unbelief. This confusion is a typical reaction for any of us at difficult times in our lives. We know God cares for us, but when we hurt, pain can cause confusion, and our hearts overpower our minds. We begin to think with our feelings.

Instead of giving into frustration because the process takes longer than we think it should, we should find Scriptures which relate to what we are dealing with and meditate on them until our faith is strengthened. It's even okay to cry out, "Lord I believe, but help my unbelief."

Exceedingly Abundantly

Are you facing an insurmountable obstacle in your life? Are your problems simply too big a challenge for you to handle? You and I face challenges every day. Usually with God's help, we can deal with them successfully. Sometimes, however, an obstacle arises which seems to defy all solutions. If you are facing one of those issues right now, I encourage you to hold on. God can handle the toughest problems confronting you.

I have encountered situations which were far more serious than the usual problems I faced. In particular, some situations way above my ability to resolve were especially stubborn and didn't want to budge, no matter how hard I tried to address them. I felt powerless. During those times, I had to depend upon Jesus and His provision to deal with it. Without fail, His power and His provision proved to be more than enough to overcome even the most difficult obstacles.

> *"Now unto Him who is able to do exceedingly abundantly above all that we ask or think, according to the power that worketh in us" (Eph. 3:20).*

When I think about this Scripture, the first detail I notice is no comma between "exceedingly" and "abundantly." Not only does God send more power and provision than we need, but He has insisted on pouring out even more bountiful measures of help. Our God works in the realm of exceeding abundance. This means there's no problem too huge for Him to solve. His ability to answer our prayers goes exceedingly abundantly beyond all we ask or think.

You see, God wants to do something far greater, far higher, and far better than anything we can imagine or think for ourselves. If we limit God to doing merely what we want, we miss out on what God wants for our lives.

Now that I've opened myself up to receive God's emotional and spiritual healing, I've learned to give all my problems, large and small, to God. This includes the problems which refuse to yield and loom like a mountain before me. If I need an abundant measure of help with a problem, I place it in His hands. It doesn't matter how much education I have; my mind can't think far enough or deep enough to ask God for all He has and can do. If I ask God for every good thing I could experience, God can do more. If I imagine things beyond my experiences, God can do more. This concept boggled my mind.

Today I stand in awe of God because His marvelous works are too wonderful for human comprehension. Now I can declare from my heart that He is able to do exceedingly abundantly beyond all that I could ask or imagine in answer to my problems.

When you allow God to take control of your problems and heal you emotionally, you can join me in shouting with a voice of jubilation.

3

Facing Adversity

Like taxes and death, adversities are unavoidable. Though many of us would rather skip them, we don't have to look upon adversities as negative experiences.

Instead of becoming discouraged and depressed, adversity can lead to our growth and development. In this chapter, I discuss some real truths about adversity and shed some light on how we can move through tough times with ease and come out better than before.

Adversity Gets Attention

Sometimes God allows adversity in our lives to get our attentions. God knows when we are too focused on ourselves and our own little worlds, so He must do something to wake us up. I have often said, there has got to be another way other than adversity to arouse us. But when things are going good in our lives, it's difficult to turn to God.

It is impossible for an unbeliever with no immediate problems to see the need for surrendering to Christ. She may feel like everything is fine and nothing needs changing. But if you go back to the same person after adversity has struck, you will find a completely different person. Tests and trials can bring even the strongest and the most stubborn of us to our knees.

Let's look at Saul, who later became the apostle Paul.

> *And as he journeyed, he came near Damascus: and*
> *suddenly there shined round about him a light from*
> *heaven: and he fell to the earth, and heard a voice*
> *saying unto him, Saul, Saul, why persecutest thou*
> *me? And he said, who art thou, Lord? And the Lord*
> *said, I am Jesus whom thou persecutest: it is hard for*
> *thee to kick against the pricks. and he trembling and*
> *astonished said, Lord, what wilt thou have me to do?*
> *And the Lord said unto him, Arise, and go into the*
> *city, and it shall be told thee what thou must do. And*
> *the men which journeyed with him stood speechless,*
> *hearing a voice, but seeing no man. And Saul arose*
> *from the earth; and when his eyes were opened, he saw*
> *no man: but they led him by the hand, and brought*
> *him into Damascus. And he was three days without*
> *sight, and neither did eat nor drink. (Acts 9:3–9).*

In this Scripture, we see how God struck Saul with a blinding light as he traveled to Damascus to arrest Christians. Since Saul thought he would not be able to see again, he was ready to listen to God. After getting his attention, Saul went on to preach about Jesus to both the Jews and the Gentiles.

Early in my Christian walk, I felt like my struggles had been unfair. Thankfully, God had me and knew exactly which buttons needed pushing. He used adversity to move me from being preoccupied with the things of this world, which drowned out his voice, to surrendering everything in my life to Him. In doing so, I could be about my Heavenly Father's business.

If you are dealing with adversity today, please know that God may be trying to get your attention. Maybe God desires to have a deeper relationship with you or He wants to prevent you from making a terrible mistake. Whatever the reason, God has a plan for your life. Sometimes He will allow adversity to move us toward fulfilling that purpose and for His will to be done.

A Nursing Student's Life

After graduating from high school, I decided to be a nurse. I had always been attracted to the nursing profession and had a desire to help sick people. Plus, it gave me the opportunity to wear those pretty crisp white uniforms nurses wore back then.

I still remember the look on my mom's face when I told her I was applying to nursing school. She looked at me as if I were someone else's child and from another planet. Without her saying a word, I knew her concern was we could not afford it. Instead of denying me the opportunity, she simply paused and said, "Okay, Arvis, I will do all I can to help you."

When I applied to nursing school and got accepted, I was elated, although this excitement didn't last long. After I received the orientation paperwork and class syllabus, knots formed in my stomach. Several students marched out of class that day. I guess they had already made up their minds they couldn't do it. I never imagined the first day of class would be tough. I had psyched myself up for the big things, like the needle sticks.

As I flipped through the syllabus, I wondered, *Lord, what have I gotten myself into?* I didn't know the answer, but I did know I wasn't going to leave. At that moment, I decided to stay and approach the course the best way I knew how, one day at a time.

Going through nursing school challenged me on many levels. Financially I struggled and made many meals out of oriental noodles and peanut butter with crackers. I thought I had good study skills, but nursing school took my studying to a place it had never been. I had never studied so long and hard. It challenged me to go deeper and higher than I knew possible. Though not easy, I stayed focused. After all, people's lives would be on the line, and I needed to know what I was doing.

I managed to make good marks, but it came with a price. Oftentimes, I would pull an all-nighter, living off coffee, trying to stuff all I could into my memory bank. My social life was pretty much nonexistent, and I missed out on a lot of partying I thought was fun. Most major exams were on Monday mornings at nine o'clock, so I usually spent the weekends tucked away studying. Because of the never-ending drugs to learn and care plans to write, among other projects, my body reacted to the stress with acne and stomach problems.

Finally, after my second year of training, I gained confidence and began to see myself as a nurse. I started counting down the months, weeks, and days until graduation. When the big day came in June of 1992, I was so relieved and thrilled I couldn't hold back tears during the graduation ceremony. Some graduates cried because they were leaving their study partners. I cried because I knew if it had not been for the Lord, I never would have made it through. At that point, I realized, though a huge investment, nursing school changed my course in life.

> *"I can do all things through Christ which strengtheneth me" (Phil. 4:13).*

Like my experience with nursing school, when faced with adversity, God is there to help us get through it. We may feel like we can't do it, and we are right. We can't do it by ourselves, but with God, we can do all things.

A Lesson in the Pain

Lessons taught in life are different than how they are taught in school. For example, in nursing school, I was taught and then tested. But life is known for testing us, then teaching us. I have learned some valuable lessons in my life, and one of those lessons taught me if you must go through pain, at least learn something from it.

I have made poor decisions, gotten involved in bad relationships, overspent, etc., and then my life became painful because I had to deal with the consequences. God is full of mercy and gave me the grace to work through those tough situations.

While experiencing the pain, I learned to humble myself and admit, "God, I missed it. I messed that up. I got in a hurry and didn't wait on you." I didn't want to be stubborn and keep going through the same pain over and over again. I knew I had to surrender to God and stop bringing pain on myself.

Yes, I wanted to let go of the past mistakes and failures. But I held on to the lessons they taught me. If I had gone through the pain and not learned anything, I would have done myself a disservice. Sooner or later, I would have to take the test again. My experience showed me if I passed the test the first time, I would not have to take the same one again and could move to the next level.

Life has an interesting way of handing out valuable lessons. Sometimes we bring pain on ourselves by our own actions, and sometimes, it's the actions of others. But our lessons are not what happens to us, rather how we respond to what happens. I have had many instructors over the years, but I will have to say pain has been one of my best teachers. I have learned much more from pain than I have ever learned from pleasure.

So, when faced with pain, I encourage you to let it teach you, not beat you!

All Things Work for Good

Although this may be easy to say, it's difficult to always believe that all things work together for our good. Remarks like this made me angry at times as they provided little consolation to me in the moment. Oftentimes, we don't think we could possibly benefit from going through adversity. We see it as a complete waste of time, which leaves us deflated and feeling used. But adversity can benefit us if we look for the good in it. Finding the good in a bad situation makes it a little bit easier to digest. We have to believe there must be something good that comes out of it. Otherwise adversity would be of no value.

Early on in my Christian walk, I had difficultly trusting God through those painful experiences, which seemed senseless and evil. I tried to hang in there and believe God would somehow turn my situation around. But I would get real annoyed at times when people tried to encourage me. As I struggled with the abuse and heartaches, some people would say things such as, "This is just a blessing in disguise" or "I bet it's just the will of God." Even to this day, I am not sure if the pain was a blessing, but I know God specializes in bringing the good out of the bad. Let's look at the life of Joseph and how God turned something bad into something meaningful and worthwhile.

> *Now Israel loved Joseph more than all his children, because he was the son of his old age: and he made him a coat of many colours. And when his brethren saw that their father loved him more than all his brethren, they hated him, and could not speak peaceably unto him . . . And it came to pass, when Joseph was come unto his brethren, that they stript Joseph out of his coat, his coat of many colours that was on him; And they took him, and cast him into a pit: and the pit was empty, there was no water in it . . . Then there passed by Midianites merchantmen; and they drew and lifted up Joseph out of the pit, and sold Joseph to the Ishmaelites for twenty pieces of silver: and they brought Joseph into Egypt. (Gen. 37:3–4, 23–24, 28).*

Joseph had a lot going for him early in life. As the firstborn son of Jacob and Rachel, he was his father's favorite. Jacob loved Joseph and gave him a coat of many colors. But when Joseph's brothers saw that their father loved Joseph more than them, they hated him and wanted to kill him. Instead, they threw him into a pit and then sold him as a slave.

At the age of seventeen, Joseph was taken to Egypt and began working for Potiphar, an officer of Pharaoh, the king of Egypt. He ended up spending a great deal of time in prison after being falsely accused by Potiphar's wife. Eventually Joseph was released from prison and brought before Pharaoh to interpret a dream. That interpretation, given to Joseph by the Lord, led to Joseph being made second in command in Egypt. Not too long afterward, a famine swept over the land. Joseph's brothers traveled to Egypt in search of food during the famine. Little did they know, they stood in the presence of their brother Joseph.

> *"And we know that all things work together for good to them that love God, to them who are the called according to his purpose" (Rom. 8:28).*

This story demonstrates how God worked everything in Joseph's life for good. He ended up saving his father and brothers by providing them a place to live in Egypt where they had food and water during the famine. Look at how God turned the whole thing around!

He is able to turn our situations around too. It may not look good right now, but God will turn everything that has been against us around for our good. Instead of being at the bottom, we will end up on top, ruling over the very things that tried so hard to stop us and keep us down.

Pulled Back to Go Further

When faced with adversity, we feel like we are being held back. Somehow, we think we're missing out on the best things in life and everyone else has passed us by. Often, we think, "Lord, this does not seem right, why do I have to wait so long?" Other people seem to come out of nowhere and achieve what we had hoped for years ago. But during these times of disappointment, we must realize we all are not on the same bus going the same speed or even going to the same place. God planned a unique journey for each of us.

When I studied an arrow, I saw a real connection in how it easily relates to life and to the nature of adversity. The arrow can easily be shot forward by being pulled back. If the arrow is not pulled back, it doesn't go very far. The farther you pull back the arrow, the farther it flies. In the same way, adversity seems to pull us back so far. We miss out on blessings, opportunities, and entire seasons. But that is rarely the case.

When the adversities of life drag you down, do not lose heart. Hold on and do not give up. God is getting ready to launch you into something great and much further than you have ever been before. God will launch you so far and so deep that you will bypass all those folks who sped by you years ago. In your season of great acceleration, God will supernaturally move you forward and bring His plans to pass at a much faster rate than humanly possible.

> *"Then said the LORD unto me, Thou hast well seen:*
> *for I will hasten my word to perform it" (Jer. 1:12).*

God is a god of acceleration and moves in our situations to bring us ahead expeditiously into our next seasons. When it's time, He speeds things up, and we find ourselves receiving long-awaited answers to prayers and experiencing spiritual advancements much sooner than we think.

That promotion, financial breakthrough, and healing you thought would take some time to come, will all change so quickly it will make your head spin.

God moves swiftly when working on our behalf.

Stay focused and aim your arrow. I promise He will allow you to hit the bull's-eye.

Pruning the Rose Bush

I love roses. I planted a rose bush in my front yard several years ago and waited for it to bloom. When the time came, it started to bloom some of the most beautiful red roses in the neighborhood. I would often bring some into the house and place them on my dining room table.

As time went by, I noticed the rose bush started to look unusual. The leaves had become yellow and lifeless. With only a few roses, the bush had grown wild and out of shape. *What in the world is this? It was so pretty just a few weeks ago.*

When I struck out to find the cause, I found out that, ever so often, a rose bush needs pruning. Pruning provides new growth, removes dead branches, lets more sunlight in, and gives the bush a better shape. I trimmed the bush quite a bit and wondered if it would survive. Weeks later, to my astonishment, the bush started to grow faster with more flowers than before. The Bible tells us about a similar process we all need to undergo if we want to grow and produce more fruit in life.

> *"Every branch in me that beareth not fruit he taketh away: and every branch that beareth fruit, he purgeth it, that it may bring forth more fruit"* *(John 15:2).*

We are all like rose bushes. God will use adversity to prune us and to weed things out of our lives. God has a greater work for us. But first He has to strip us of the things which are not needed and keep us from being productive. I know pruning hurts, and sometimes it may look like we are not going to make it. Thankfully, God is the master gardener, and He knows how to cut out the dead things which are not useful in advancing His kingdom. When He is done pruning and getting rid of fleshly things, we will grow and bloom bigger and better than ever.

The Valley of Despair

Facing adversity compares to being in a valley or a tough place where we feel all alone. Valley life offers many challenges and battles. Low and unpleasant, the valley is a place where we struggle with hopes, fears, and painful circumstances.

People find themselves in the valley for various reasons. It may be spiritual warfare, the actions of others, their own actions, or even the hand of God. But one thing is for certain, we all have to go through the valley. It's not a matter of "if," it's a matter of "when."

When I wandered into the valley of despair, I felt lonely. During those dark and dreary days, I felt as if no one cared. I wanted to go back on the mountaintop. But in life, there's usually a valley experience after the mountaintop. The valley life presented hardships and frustrations. People judged unfairly, but God came to my rescue. He's not just God of the mountaintop. He is also God of the valley. As I struggled during my time in the valley, King David assured me I could make it through.

> *"Yea, though I walk through the valley of the shadow*
> *of death, I will fear no evil: for thou art with me;*
> *thy rod and thy staff they comfort me" (Ps. 23:4).*

The valley is meant to be a temporary place. We are to walk through the valley, not take up residence there. Some people have been in the valley for so long, getting up has never crossed their minds.

It may seem difficult and like you can't just get up and walk out. But you can get back on top if you surrender to God and believe He will walk by your side, especially during trials.

Dropping the Baggage

I have held on to so many things from my past such as bad memories, heartbreaks, and major disappointments. Whenever I tried to do something positive and worthwhile, those dark memories would crawl out to remind me of the past, making sure I would never forget those terrible things.

One day, I got fed up and came to a fork in the road. I had to make a choice. I could either hold on to my old baggage and stay bound or drop the baggage and break free. I chose to let go of the baggage that weighed me down and embrace freedom. Without realizing it, I had carried that baggage with me everywhere I went. I shared it with family, friends, co-workers, church members, etc. Finally, I decided to accept my past and fully acknowledge it couldn't be changed. But I could change how I looked at it and not allow it to control my life anymore.

> *"If the Son therefore shall make you free, ye shall be*
> *free indeed" (John 8:36).*

In order to be free, I had to trust God to make right all the wrongs in my past. Exercising my faith was not to strengthen my grip but to strengthen my release. I had to release all the junk which had built up over the years. It wasn't good to go through life carrying all that negative pressure around with me. When I released my painful past to God, He set me free from the twisted thoughts I had been holding on to since childhood. At that point, I got to BE free, both in my mind and my heart.

Once we can let the past go, we will be able to soar like an eagle. The choice is ours. We can either choose to allow the hurts, wounds, and pains from our pasts to continue to smother and squeeze the life out of us, or we can choose to say, "I have had enough," and surrender our pasts to God. His power and healing are right there for us to grasp. But first, we have to drop the baggage, take His hand, and allow Him to bring us up and out of it.

The Ashes of Adversity

When I was a young girl, I often watched my mother cook. One day while observing her cooking skills, I saw her bury some sweet potatoes in the hot ashes of our wood-burning stove. I remember wondering if those potatoes would be suitable to eat after being cooked in ashes. After they finished baking, I found my answer. Those baked potatoes looked bad on the outside, but they were delicious on the inside. They were so good I ate two or three at one sitting.

> *"To appoint unto them that mourn in Zion, to give unto them beauty for ashes, the oil of joy for mourning, the garment of praise for the spirit of heaviness; that they might be called trees of righteousness, the planting of the LORD, that he might be glorified" (Isa. 61:3).*

"Thou preparest a table before me in the presence of mine enemies: thou anointest my head with oil; my cup runneth over" (Ps. 23:5).

In due season, God is going to deliver us from under all the dust and grime from our pasts and place us on a table for all to see His marvelous works on display. God will prepare a table before us in the presence of our enemies. Often, we are so busy looking at our enemies, and we don't look at the table. Just like my mom brought those potatoes out of the ashes, God will take our "ashy" situations and turn them into something beautiful.

Looking Back

God has an amazing plan for each of us and wants to use our pasts for His purpose. But we can't accomplish His plan if we continue looking in the rearview mirror. Looking back only delays what God has for us and can even be fatal.

When God decided to destroy the cities of Sodom and Gomorrah due to their wickedness, He sent angels to warn Lot to take his family and to hurry up and leave Sodom.

"And it came to pass, when they had brought them forth abroad, that he said, Escape for thy life; look not behind thee, neither stay thou in all the plain; escape to the mountain, lest thou be consumed" (Gen. 19:17).

The angels warned them not to look back, but Lot's wife hungered for the experiences of the past. She craved the things of Sodom. Lot's family was so caught up in the city's culture, the angels had to take them by the hands and lead them safely away as the brimstone rained down. As they escaped, Lot's wife looked back, and she became a pillar of salt. Lot's wife was destroyed with the city because she ignored the warning sign.

"But his wife looked back from behind him, and she became a pillar of salt" (Gen. 19:26).

We can't move forward in faith if we keep looking back at our pasts.

"Brethren, I count not myself to have apprehended: but this one thing I do, forgetting those things which are behind, and reaching forth unto those things which are before, I press toward the mark for the prize of the high calling of God in Christ Jesus" (Phil. 3:13–14).

We all have regrets and disappointments that seem to haunt us and dampen our hopes for the future. Paul looked back over his life with the realization of many disappointments, unmet goals, and unrealized dreams. Rather than fade away into regrets, he embraced a forward leaning position.

I look back with many regrets regarding my life—ruined relationships, destroyed friendships, lost opportunities, and bitter failures. If we're not careful, harmful emotions can form from these disappointments, and we can become miserable in our present circumstances, which hinder us in the future.

When I made a conscious effort to forget those things in my past, I began to progress in life. I finally stopped falling back on all the bad things which had occurred. No longer did I use those things to justify some of the foolish things I did. Just because I may have come from a dysfunctional family, did not imply I had to be dysfunctional and live a reckless life. I did not want to look back and die, rather I wanted to look forward and live. I pressed toward the mark of the high calling of God.

God has a higher calling for us. But we will miss our callings unless we heed to His warning, "Don't look back."

4

Wounds of Rejection

When we love or desperately need someone, and they are not there for us, we feel rejected. Rejection is when someone or something refuses to accept us, or we sense we're not loved or wanted. Rejection commonly occurs in the world today, but many people do not fully understand the basic concept and how it affects an individual.

All of us have been rejected at some point in life, but if we do not handle rejection properly, it can cause deep gouges. These wounds can be so deep, painful, and shattering that they can affect our entire lives and all our relationships.

Personally, rejection reminds me of the times I worked in the tool factory during the summer. When the tools did not past inspections, we placed them in a "reject bin" to be thrown away.

My rejection experience inflicted a lot of emotional pain, and I spent many days wondering if I could get through it. It's difficult when you have been rejected by someone you trusted and shared secrets and struggles with. Rejection from loved ones can be devastating. In my case, trust had been violated, and I felt betrayed. The pain of betrayal intensified because I ended up feeling vulnerable since the foundation of trust had been broken. Situations like these left deep wounds which initially I didn't recognize. As life went on, I realized something was seriously wrong with me. Those wounds of rejection cut deep, and I lived in fear of being hurt again. But God was there for me.

> *"When my father and my mother forsake me, then*
> *the LORD will take me up" (Ps. 27:10).*

If you feel rejected, rejoice and be glad because the Lord will receive you. If you have been thrown out like trash, don't lose hope, the Lord will take you in. Your spouse may abandon you for someone else, but the Lord will receive you. Don't worry when rejection comes your way, be glad because the Lord is tracking you down with wide open arms to receive you.

Childhood Rejection

There are many causes of rejection, but one of the major causes is not feeling loved by parents, especially the father. Why the father? Well, the father is crucial to the emotional well-being of the child, and a child can't completely be secure without proper love from a father. A person who has not received proper love from a father exposes themselves to the wounds of rejection.

Children are especially vulnerable to the damages caused by rejection because they are still developing identity and learning who they are. Parents and authority figures can deeply wound us, because we look up to them and rely on them.

Personally, I began to experience rejection early in my childhood although I did not fully grasp what was happening. I guess I had a high degree of sensitivity, and certain things bothered me at a young age. Living with an alcoholic father caused me a lot of confusion and mixed emotions. I knew my father loved me. He just had a strange way of showing his love. He was a good provider. We always had food to eat and a roof over our heads. In the winter months, he made sure we always had a huge supply of wood available for our wood heater. My father would cut wood and stack it a mile high on the porch.

Though small in stature, he somehow managed to lift those huge wooden logs onto his back.

All of this was great, and I thank God for how my father provided for me. But there were still some things I desperately needed from him such as his attention and acceptance. The alcohol affected my father's ability to communicate effectively and to socialize properly. These things drove a wedge between us and caused a major strain on our relationship. There were many times when I needed to talk to him and get his advice, but fear overpowered my motivation to approach him. When under the influence of alcohol, he was not pleasant to be around. This type of behavior left me feeling alone, rejected, abandoned, and hurt.

Childhood rejection became problematic for me. As I continued through life, I was exposed to even more rejection when I became involved in close relationships. Some of those relationships didn't work well because I looked for someone to fill the hole in my heart left from childhood.

Why Does Rejection Wound Us So Deeply?

Before I answer the question of why rejection wounds so deeply, let's first look at how human beings were made. This may seem a bit off course, but hopefully you will see the connection soon.

> "And God said, let us make man in our image, after our likeness: and let them have dominion over the fish of the sea, and over the fowl of the air, and over the cattle, and over all the earth, and over every creeping thing that creepeth upon the earth" (Gen. 1:26).

> "God is a Spirit: and they that worship him must worship him in spirit and in truth" (John 4:24).

Scripture tells us that man was made in the image of God, and God is a spirit. This means all human beings are first and foremost spirits, not bodies. On the inside of every living human body dwells a human spirit. That is the real person, the one created in the image of God. We are spiritual beings having human experiences on the earth. Now that we know we are spiritual beings, we can understand fully why rejection wounds us so deeply.

The rejections I encountered in life caused such pain and heartache. I wanted to block them out of my mind. I found it almost impossible not to dwell on them because, deep down, I knew I felt that way for a reason but didn't know why. As I began to study Scripture, I realized the rejection was not in my mind, but my spirit. This type of damage to the spirit is described in Scripture.

"A merry heart maketh a cheerful countenance: but by sorrow of the heart the spirit is broken" (Prov. 15:13).

A lively and vibrant spirit helps us through great trials and sickness, but a crushed spirit will have a debilitating effect in all areas of our lives. Rejection wounds us deeply because it affects our spirits, which define us. We may end up looking good but feeling bad. For being rejected cuts to the core and causes us to be miserable, no matter how attractive our appearance or how much our clothes cost. But if we continue on the rejected path, eventually a crushed spirit will have a negative impact on our bodies, right down to our bones.

"A merry heart doeth good like a medicine: but a broken spirit drieth the bones" (Prov. 17:22).

When we look at these negative responses to rejection, it's hard to understand why people cause others such pain. Have you ever heard someone say, "Hurt people hurt people?" People are usually motivated to do what they do because of the deep and hidden hurts in their lives. Their bad behaviors prevent them from being hurt again and provide a way for them to deal with their pains. When we understand this, the reasons people do certain things will actually begin to make sense. Rejection hurts, and people often go to extreme measures to prevent the possibility of being rejected again.

Building Walls

After feeling the horrible pain of rejection, I decided to take matters into my own hands by building a wall of protection. Now I have never been much of a builder. The only thing I have ever built is a bridge from pop-sickle sticks in grade school. Somehow, I managed to build a wall of protection around my heart. I had made up my mind I was not going to ever allow anyone else to get close to me and hurt me. I figured people couldn't hurt me if they were not allowed to get close. I reminded myself I couldn't trust anyone and promised myself I would never go through such pain again.

Admittedly it sounded awfully good to say I was taking matters into my own hands, but here lies the truth. It didn't take long for me to realize this placed me in a dangerous position. I soon discovered the walls I built and bragged about were not real and didn't work.

To me, my walls appeared real because I conjured them up in my mind. But in reality, self-made walls only provided a false sense of security. It didn't take away my fears or relieve my pain, it only covered them up, so people could not see them. On the inside, I was still wounded.

My walls didn't keep me from getting hurt but prevented me from freely receiving love as God intended. While blocking everyone out of my life, I ended up keeping Jesus from reaching the wounds of my heart that desperately needed healing. When I finally began to realize my walls weren't working in my favor, I began to take them down. Now I thank God for breaking down the barriers that held me captive. Those things which towered over me and held me tight gradually began to fall.

> *"And the LORD said unto Joshua, See, I have given into thine hand Jericho, and the king thereof, and the mighty men of valour" (Josh. 6:2).*

When I became ready, God gave me the victory over the Jerichos in my life. He broke down the barriers, the hedges, and the walls, making a way for Him to heal me.

I don't have to depend on a wall any longer. I can depend on God. His unfailing love closed every gap the enemy used as an access against me. Now I can experience the freedom God intended for me. God rescued me, and I have a newfound confidence to move forward with Jesus leading the way.

Striving for Perfection

Perfectionism is another behavior people use to counter rejection. Perfectionism refers to a set of unrealistic thoughts and behaviors aimed at reaching extremely high goals. We live in a world that praises and celebrates perfectionism. Our society values ambition, zeal, and a constant drive to better oneself. While these things can be good, they can spin out of control into perfectionism, where we end up striving for the unattainable and the unreachable.

Over the years, I attempted to hide the pain of rejection by burying it behind my achievements, awards, and degrees. I wanted to be accepted and recognized, so I worked tirelessly to prove my worth. Rather than just working toward success, I ended up trying to be perfect and tried protecting myself from criticism. This caused me to value myself based on other people's approval, which became a practice, since my worth depended on others' opinions. Also, my self-defeating thoughts led me to believe I could come to know everything or at least know more than the next person. Ultimately, these unhealthy thought patterns negatively affected my self-esteem.

The most important thing to remember about perfectionism is that it comes from a place of fear. It's a distorted view which says, "If I do everything perfectly, I can avoid rejection and all of the hurtful feelings which come with it." Perfectionism comes from fear of failure, disapproval, and making mistakes. But where did this spirit of fear come from?

"For God hath not given us the spirit of fear; but of power, and of love, and of a sound mind" (2 Tim. 1:7).

This type of fear doesn't come from God, rather the enemy. Satan puts fear in us, causing us to set unrealistic goals which are impossible to reach. When these goals are not met, pressure rises. The increased pressure leads to anxiety, exhaustion, and depression. It's an endless report card on accomplishments and a sure way to a life of sadness and destruction.

In reality, Jesus is the only perfect one. Instead of striving for flawlessness, I decided to stay centered on the Lord. I no longer wanted to be like that hamster on the wheel, going around and around, trying to do more and get more, but not going anywhere.

Sometimes we may wonder why people would go through such trouble to build walls and try to be perfect. Again, these behaviors develop to avoid further hurt, as well as deal with existing pain.

Thankfully, we can turn away from the pain and toward God. He knows all of our mistakes and mishaps but loves us anyway. None of us are perfect and never will be. But God is perfect, and His love for us covers our imperfections through His grace.

Love Takes Pain Away

I believe one of the most devastating effects rejection causes is the inability to receive love and to love others. An individual who has never experienced love struggles with passing on love to someone else. We can't really love ourselves until we know how much God loves us, and if we don't love ourselves, we can't love other people. It's impossible to maintain healthy relationships without a foundation of love.

Suffering from rejection left me desperate for love. I went looking for it in all the wrong places and made plenty of mistakes along the way. When I finally found love, I didn't know how to receive it. My husband, Carl, tried to love me, but I was so broken during the early phases of our relationship, I constantly avoided his love and acts of kindness. Due to the way I felt about myself, I deflated his love.

As I established a relationship with God, I came to learn about God's unconditional love, and I eventually began to accept my husband's love and God's love. I began to say, "God loves me, and I receive His love." I said this over and over until it penetrated my heart. It felt good to feel God's love, and it has brought me so much comfort. As I developed a love relationship with God, I had no room left for rejection and fear. I realized God not only loved me, but He would also send other people who would love me, too.

"We love him, because he first loved us" (1 John 4:19).

The proof of my healing from rejection came through God giving me divine love for people who had rejected me.

How about you? Can you go back to an unloving parent or family member and say, "I love you?" Now I even say a prayer for my enemies and ask God to bless them. I know it's the most unnatural thing in the world to do, but God's love is not natural. It's supernatural, far above anything that precedes our own efforts.

If you ask God to help you, He will give you the grace to do it. Think about it. You can be a vessel of love to others by helping to take pain away from those who have also been rejected. No greater blessing follows healing than this.

The Ultimate Rejection

Though painful, my rejection didn't compare to the rejection Jesus experienced. Jesus received rejection from man and even from God. First, let's see how Jesus was rejected by man.

> *"Therefore the Jews sought the more to kill him, because he not only had broken the Sabbaths, but said also that God was his Father, making himself equal with God" (John 5:18).*

The Jews rejected Jesus, but even worse than that, His close friends deserted Him. One even denied Him.

> *"But all this was done, that the scriptures of the prophets might be fulfilled. Then all the disciples forsook him, and fled" (Matt. 26:56).*

> *"And after a while came unto him they that stood by, and said to Peter, Surely thou also art one of them; for thy speech betrayeth thee. Then began he to curse and to swear, saying, I know not the man. And immediately the cock crew" (Matt. 26:73–74).*

As if the rejection of men wasn't bad enough, Jesus went on to experience an even more cruel experience. Let's look at what Jesus went through on the cross.

> *Now from the sixth hour there was darkness over all the land unto the ninth hour. And about the ninth hour Jesus cried with a loud voice, saying, Eli, Eli, lama sabachthani? That is to say, My God, my God, why hast thou forsaken me? Some of them that stood there, when they heard that, said, this man calleth for Elias. And straightway one of them ran, and took a sponge, and filled it with vinegar, and put it on a reed, and gave him to drink. The rest said, Let be, let us see whether Elias will come to save him. Jesus, when he had cried again with a loud voice, yielded up the ghost. (Matt. 27:45–50).*

In this passage of Scripture, we see Jesus praying to God, but God does not answer. Since Jesus came to die for our sins, the rejection and pain were necessary for Jesus to endure. After He died, look at what happened.

> *"And, behold, the veil of the temple was rent in twain from the top to the bottom; and the earth did quake, and the rocks rent" (Matt. 27:51).*

This means the wall between God and man had been removed, and we now have a direct route to God. We can go to Him without fear. Jesus went through the ultimate rejection, so we can experience God's acceptance.

Accepted into the Family

We can't place more value into lost outcomes than we do into God's purposes. Life is not about living an endless procession of disappointments and pain. Jesus took our pain. He was rejected so we could be accepted. He bore our grief, so we could live in increasing joy every day. Jesus provided for our release from the graveyard of pain and rejection.

Even before creation, God's purpose has been for us to become His sons and daughters. When Jesus died on the cross, He opened the way for our acceptance. God says, "Come on in, welcome to the family." Jesus took our rejection on the cross, along with all the hurt and pain.

> *Blessed be the God and Father of our Lord Jesus Christ, who hath blessed us with all spiritual blessings in heavenly places in Christ: According as he hath chosen us in him before the foundation of the world, that we should be holy and without blame before him in love: Having predestinated us unto the adoption of children by Jesus Christ to himself, according to the good pleasure of his will, To the praise of the glory of his grace, wherein he hath made us accepted in the beloved. (Eph. 1:3–6).*

Jesus took the bad, so we might receive the good. What a glorious exchange!

All we have to do is accept Christ's death and resurrection to be part of God's family. Even when our families mistreat us, our father rejects us, our mother never has time for us, or our spouse never expresses love to us, God loves us and wants us to be in fellowship with Him. We may have unpleasant memories of our biological fathers, but we still have a Heavenly Father who loves us and will never leave us.

Protection May Look Like Rejection

Joseph's brothers thought they had gotten rid of him by selling Joseph to slave traders in a foreign country. In reality, God protected Joseph by getting the brothers out of his life. Joseph probably looked at the situation and thought they were rejecting him, but really God was protecting him. What may look like rejection in your life can be protection.

Joseph had to be separated from his brothers in order for God to protect His call and destiny. Joseph was going places he had never been. He went from the bottom to the top, from the prison to the palace, from poverty to prosperity, and his brothers were not able to go with him at the time. He had to be separated from his family to become who God wanted him to be. But God took everything Joseph went through and worked it out in His favor. Many of us, just like Joseph, have gone through trying times. And, just like Joseph, God will change our situations, but first He has to separate us, so He can protect us.

Unmasking the Pain

The world can be a bruising place for rejected people. A regular day can be emotionally draining. Our human nature puts us on lookout to avoid being rejected. We'll do anything to avoid the pain of being judged, left out, or rejected again.

One option is to wear a mask to get through the day and to hide how we really feel. Sometimes when people rob a bank or commit a crime they wear a mask, so no one can see how they look. Wearing an emotional mask prevents people from seeing the real you. They only see the person you allow them to see.

Wearing a beauty mask doesn't cost much, but the cost of wearing an emotional mask is high. While masking pain may provide protection in the short run, over time, we become somewhat isolated. We end up missing out on real relationships with others because they fall in love with the mask, or we are afraid to allow them to get close enough to see what's under it.

I put on my mask in childhood, and it became bigger as I aged. My first experience with rejection crushed my feelings. I was too young to defend myself and ended up being humiliated. For protection, I started wearing a mask and didn't let anyone in. I behaved as if I were happy all the time. No one knew when my feelings were hurt, and to the outside world, nothing got me down. I joked and smiled even when my personal life screamed chaos. I pretended to be strong when everything churned in turmoil on the inside. I had moments when my troubles seemed big and my faith small. I wore several different masks, although my true identity hid behind pain, fear, and confusion.

Coping with everything life threw my way proved tough. Playing a pretending game drained my mind and body as I tried to hide my real self. Constantly pretending to be someone else took its toll, especially when I began rejecting the way I felt. I became physically exhausted trying to hold up the mask.

Finally, I stepped out of denial and called it what it really was, "rejection." I threw the mask away, and once I got real with myself, healing began. I no longer needed to be strong or pretend everything was okay. I could be myself and be vulnerable, for I came to realize God accepts me even when I am weak.

"For we have not an high priest which cannot be touched with the feeling of our infirmities; but was in all points tempted like as we are, yet without sin.

Let us therefore come boldly unto the throne of grace, that we may obtain mercy, and find grace to help in time of need" (Heb. 4:15–16).

God will not reject us because of our weaknesses and mistakes. God loves us and accepts us because of who He is, not because of who we are or what we have done.

Will you be vulnerable enough to take off your mask? Your mask is not who you are. Don't waste the rest of your life pretending to be someone or something other than you. Your healing lies in putting down the mask and being seen. Restoration resides in removing the mask and facing the hidden hurts deep in your heart. God knows you are weak, and He still wants to help you. He wants to shine the light on your pain and heal you from past hurts caused by rejection.

5

Offense, Resentment, and Bitterness

What happens to us is not nearly as important as how we react. If we do not become offended and resent the person or situation, chances are it will do us little harm. However, if we allow the matter to cause us to be offended, resentful, and bitter, it can cause a lot of harm. The negative emotions of offenses, resentment, and bitterness work together and can wreak havoc on an individual's life if not handled properly.

Through practice, I learned to confront my being offended when it snuck into view, immediately closing the door on resentment and bitterness which typically follow.

Get Behind Me Satan

Many people are not able to function properly because of their hurts and offenses. Hurt people easily offend, as their judgment is cloudy, and they rush to conclusions without getting all the information. Satan knows this, which is why causing us to become offended remains one of his top strategies. He then draws us into resentment and bitterness. Offense serves as a stumbling block which keeps us from entering into God's blessings.

All of us have been offended at some time or another. Offense didn't seem to bother me as much when I was in the world, but when I decided to follow the Lord, it looked as if offense waited for me on every corner. All kinds of people who just didn't seem to be on the same page with me confronted me. I always got angry, hurt, or upset.

When minimizing the impact of offense, some people may say, "That was an insult," or "They really rubbed me the wrong way." But it all means they were offended. I had to learn to identify offense as one of Satan's traps to stop me from going to the next level God had for me. I developed boldness and told Satan to leave me alone because he couldn't stop me any longer. I followed the example of Jesus in how he dealt with offense.

> *"But he turned, and said unto Peter, get thee behind me, Satan: thou art an offence unto me: for thou savourest not the things that be of God, but those that be of men" (Matt. 16:23).*

When Jesus told the disciples He would be crucified, Peter immediately told Jesus to stop talking in such a way. Peter didn't understand the next level of Jesus's ministry. Jesus told Peter to "get behind me, Satan" for he was an offense to Him. In other words, Peter was a stumbling block, a hindrance to the Master's work. Jesus fed the multitudes and healed the sick, but the cross beckoned His ultimate destiny.

Yes, people can be rude sometimes, treat you unkindly, and do things to try to hinder you from moving into the things of God. Don't get angry and act out of character. Just tell them what Jesus told Peter, "Get behind me, Satan."

The Best Defense for Offense

Opportunities to be offended abound. Every day we may encounter people who say things or do something which does not sit well with us. Oftentimes, people leave home defensive as if they expect to be offended before the end of the day.

The truth of the matter is, we don't actually have to be offended unless we allow it. If we never pick up the offense, then our hearts will not suffer from the effects of it. To be offended is a choice we make, rather than a condition imposed upon us by someone else. We can choose to be offended and feed our hurts until they destroy us, or we can choose not to be offended.

Previously, I must have been the most easily offended person in the world. I used to walk in bondage with hurt feelings. Yes, I loved the Lord, but I struggled with submitting my feelings to Him. Extremely sensitive, I was thin-skinned and spent a huge chunk of time feeling hurt and upset at people or circumstances. My sensitivity caused me a lot of pain and discomfort.

I often walked around with a chip on my shoulder, quick to misinterpret things. I failed to realize my own touchiness and lost my joy because I was so easily offended. I felt slighted by what others said or did to me. Some of this touchiness came from my unique personality. But choosing to be offended also meant I had a more serious issue. I harbored unforgiveness, deep hurts, and scars which needed healing. I couldn't live in a glass bottle or bubble in an effort to avoid being offended. There had to be a way for me to rise above the drama.

After researching it, I realized the Bible has a game plan to help us defend ourselves against these traps. If we stick to the plan which has been laid out for us, we can still interact with others and resist offensive behavior.

"Great peace has they which love thy law: and nothing shall offend them" (Ps. 119:165).

Those who love God's law by accepting His Word as true will have great peace in this world, and this peace will keep them from becoming offended. Peaceful folks have "think skin" and know how to survive letdowns and disappointments from others.

Through studying Scripture, I have learned to choose my battles and have chosen not to fight with offense. I can't afford to be offended for another minute. I now give people the benefit of the doubt and am no longer easily provoked.

Resenting the Past

If we allow offense to linger, sooner or later, we become resentful. Being resentful is damaging because we rehearse the harmful and painful situation over and over in our hearts. Resentment harbors a deep feeling of anger, a grudge, or painful memories of past hurts. It's a sin and deadly poison which causes struggles for many. Resentment seems to be caused by what happened to us, but it is really caused by how we related to what happened.

When I struggled with resentment, a major part of me shut down. I lost my joy and zeal for life. Unable to express love, I made things difficult. I resented my past and other people because they were the reason for most of my pains and heartaches. In other words, they were my problems, not me. I blamed other people, so I wouldn't have to look at myself.

Hurting people don't want to look at themselves as being difficult. If they do, they have to deal with what happened. I didn't want to feel unworthy of being loved and not being good enough. To avoid this hurt, I resented.

I knew if I wanted to release resentment, I had to be willing to feel the hurt which was ruining my life. I had to address my feelings of not being good enough and not worth loving. I realized if I experienced the hurt, I would no longer need resentment, but the pain ached badly enough already. Why subject myself to further pain? I guess I wasn't quite ready to let go of the resentment nor heal the hurt.

Holding Grudges

Resentment can be harmful as it destroys relationships. More damaging, however, is how it destroys people holding on to grudges, refusing to let go. They don't realize they carry bags filled with pain and misery, which penetrate the heart. Holding a grudge bottles an irritation until it explodes into full-blown hatred. Grudges can last for a long time, even years, causing us to rewind our past, which prevents us from moving forward.

At one time in my life, I held on to grudges. Since I had been offended and had become resentful, I felt justified. Since I had built a false image of the other person, I was able to push aside the big picture, which included the good things they had done, and only dwell on their wrongdoings.

Also, I liked to keep score by playing a game of tit-for-tat, where I counted the number of times someone mistreated me. I often responded with, "This isn't the first time you have done this, but who's counting?" Since I knew exactly how many times they had wronged me, at the time, I felt I had every reason in the world to hold a grudge. In doing so, I managed to keep my hurts alive and feel sorry for myself. I usually didn't reach satisfaction until everyone else felt sorry for me too. Their empathy satisfied my craving for attention. Resentment is meant to punish the other person but was far more hurtful to me than it could have ever been to anyone else. In most cases, the other person was not even aware of having done anything wrong. Therefore, my resentment did not hurt them at all. Instead, it stripped me of loving relationships.

I held grudges because I didn't want to let people off the hook. I wanted them to know how bad I hurt. If I walked around not speaking to someone and not treating them right, then I was hurting them, right? Not at all. Now I see how I was handcuffed to my past. I thought I held the grudge, but really the grudge held me!

What does God say about grudges?

"Thou shalt not avenge, nor bear any grudge against the children of thy people, but thou shalt love thy neighbour as thyself: I am the LORD" (Lev. 19:18).

God has such a strong concern about grudges He included a specific command about them. God says He is the Lord. To hold a grudge sets us up as judge. So, if we keep a grudge, we are doubting the judge. When we look at grudges in this sense, we realize we don't have the right to determine someone else's fate. We only keep ourselves in bondage by remaining tied to the past. Grudges leave when we release our hurtful feelings to the Lord alone. When doing so, we feel so much better because we have relinquished our free wills and given the Lord permission to handle our situations as He sees fit.

I don't know about you, but I'm pretty sure God can do a much better job with my affairs than I can!

Bitter Feelings

Those feelings of resentment eventually took a toll on me. I had focused all my attention on one individual and soon became bitter because I kept holding on and wouldn't let it go. The word *bitterness* means something with a sharp taste or lack of sweetness.

A true Southerner, I love mustard and turnip greens. I can't think of too many more food items I love to eat more. There is nothing like a huge plate of greens with cornbread. But every now and then, I come across a plate of bitter greens. The sharp bitter taste causes me to frown and push the plate back. Bitterness causes a similar reaction in the spiritual realm. It not only causes physical discomfort in us, it also causes discomfort to the Holy Spirit who dwells within us.

In my life, people have hurt me, taken advantage of me, rejected me, and taken credit for the work I have done. People have even tried to belittle me in order to enlarge themselves. Instead of forgiving them, I became resentful and bitter. But the Bible tells us we are to be sweet to those with whom we come in contact.

"For we are unto God a sweet savour of Christ, in them that are saved, and in them that perish" (2 Cor. 2:15).

According to the above Scripture, we should release an aroma which is sweet smelling and attractive. When filled with bitterness, it's impossible to be sweet. Bitterness pollutes the environment and releases deadly toxins. A bitter person is not easy to be around. We must live in a way which produces the sweet aroma of Christ, for His fragrance brings life to the hurting and dying.

The Root of Bitterness

Before a root can grow, a seed has to be planted. When someone does us wrong or when we perceive we were wronged, a bitter seed can be planted, and we become angry toward others instead of forgiving. When we don't forgive, we handle the hurt inappropriately, and the root of bitterness creeps into our lives. Oftentimes we don't even know it's there until we start feeling some type of discomfort.

One morning I woke up around two o'clock with a horrible toothache. I got up, took a couple of pain pills, and waited for the dentist's office to open at eight o'clock. When I arrived, I had an x-ray which detected my pain's source. My tooth was cracked in several places at the root. Now I couldn't see anything wrong with the tooth. On the surface it looked fine, but the cracks in the root of my tooth were so great and the pain throbbed so badly, it disturbed my sleep. The root of bitterness works the same way. You may not see the root, but it's there, and when you least expect it, it will shoot up and cause a lot of aches and pain.

"Looking diligently lest any man fail of the grace of God; lest any root of bitterness springing up trouble you, and thereby many be defiled" (Heb. 12:15).

Oftentimes the person who hurts us does it unintentionally; other times it's on purpose. In either situation, a seed is planted, sprouts, and takes root. No one can see the root because it lies beneath the surface, invisible to the eye. Though out of sight, the root of the issue remains in our lives. Its presence is real and will shoot forth, causing pain and other trouble when we least expect it.

Collateral Damage

One thing we know for certain about a root, it grows. The root of bitterness spreads quickly and causes problems for many people. Collateral damage occurs when bitterness becomes destructive to a person and those around her. When a person harbors anger and bitterness, an overflow of feelings and reactions occur. Since people don't know where to put their hurts, those around them become perfect targets for their pain. Maybe you have worked with such a person, or you may be married to a bitter person. If you are not careful, bitterness can penetrate the entire room.

Bitterness is often driven by feeling someone must take the blame. I figured if I could put the blame on someone else, my pain would get better and may even disappear altogether. I often released my painful feelings—meant for someone else—onto the safest people I knew, my family and friends. I fell into the trap of murmuring and complaining, the voices of bitterness. I didn't know why I couldn't be happy like everyone else. I grumbled and criticized everything. I wanted people to just leave me alone, and that is exactly what they did. My grumbling drove a wedge between me and those who loved me. Living in a state of bitterness can be lonely, for who wants to be around such a person?

Bitterness causes collateral damage, spreading like poison if left unattended. When I harbored bitterness in my heart, my marriage began failing before I knew it. I wasn't speaking to others, and most of my other relationships also suffered. Finally, I realized hurting others with my pain and emotions was no way to live. I couldn't go on flooding other people with my tender feelings. I had to learn how to deal with my bitterness.

Getting Rid of Bitterness

We know bitterness can cause a lot of trouble for us, but what can be done about it? Do we keep it inside and continue to make ourselves sick, physically, emotionally, and spiritually? Do we release our bitter feelings onto others and make everyone else sick? Or do we get rid of bitterness by digging up the root?

Before I could get rid of bitterness, I had to recognize and confess I held resentment for other people. I had to accept bitterness as my problem and not the problem of the people who offended me. Bitterness is the sin of the bitter person, no matter what sin the offender has done. My bitterness didn't develop because of what somebody did to me, I was bitter because I chose to be offended. If I wanted the root of bitterness to stop growing in my life, I had to stop focusing on the people who hurt me and start focusing on my bitterness as a sin. Once I did this, bitterness had to go and could no longer control my life.

When we played in the yard as children, and if one of us picked up a stick, my father would tell us, "Put that stick down before somebody gets hurt." That is exactly what I had to do with my bitterness. I had to get rid of it before its deadly root did me harm and caused a lot of pain.

> *"Let all bitterness, and wrath, and anger, and clamour, and evil speaking, be put away from you, with all malice" (Eph. 4:31).*

In His Word, God tells us to put bitterness away, along with its friends of wrath, anger, and evil talk. I decided to listen to God's wise counsel and pulled bitterness up by its root and out of my mind. Although not easy, I got rid of bitterness and refused to allow its root to grow another inch in my life.

6

Me and My Anger

What makes you angry? Are they small things such as long lines in grocery stores or not being able to find a shoe? Or are they bigger things, like experiencing injustices or violence? How do you deal with your anger? Does everyone around you know when and why you are angry? Or do you turn your anger in on yourself and become depressed?

We can't avoid dealing with anger. Anger is a response to living in a troubled world where things can and do go wrong. But, if we don't learn how to deal with our anger, we will constantly hurt ourselves and others.

Anger functions as our God-given capacity to respond to a wrong we think is important and matters to us. Anger can be viewed as a strong emotion, and if mishandled, it can make us want to hurt somebody. Mishandled anger remains a big issue, but not the primary one. It simply acts as a warning light on our dashboards which says something under the hood is wrong.

I have struggled in dealing with my anger. When I hurt, sometimes I would make myself angry because I would rather deal with the anger than to deal with the pain. Other times, I tried to act like nothing bothered me, but the pain I experienced kept bubbling up to the surface. Every time I thought about my past, I boiled over with deep, burning anger. I thought about how I could get even with the people who angered me.

When those feelings swept over me, I didn't know where they came from and how to handle them. When I tried to hide them, I got all knotted up inside. When I tried to express them, by "getting it off my chest," people ended up deeply wounded. *So which is it? Do I vent my angry feelings or calm myself down?*

Stuffing our anger deep inside destroys our mental well-beings. Our anger needs to be acknowledged and expressed in a positive way. At the same time, venting anger and hurting everyone involved is inappropriate. God has a different way for us to deal with our anger. His approach makes it possible for us to express anger in a way that truly saves challenging situations and relationships.

Wanting It More Than God

I want good things in life. I want my children to respect and obey me. It's not wrong to want my husband to love and listen to me. It's not wrong to want my friends to be honest with me. But if these things become more important than anything else, then I want them too much. When we don't get what we want or believe we need and deserve, the wrong type of anger flares.

> *"From whence come wars and fightings among you? Come they not hence, even of your lusts that war in your members? Ye lust, and have not: ye kill, and desire to have, and cannot obtain: ye fight and war, yet ye have not, because ye ask not" (James 4:1–2).*

James tells us anger comes when we can't have our way about something. Since we can't have it, we argue and fight. When we want anything, even a good thing more than God, we will get angry when we don't get it or when it is taken away from us.

Wrong Ways to Express Anger

When I used to get angry, my problem was not my anger, the problem existed in how I expressed it. God gave us anger as a way to point out when something is wrong. Since we live in a world filled with reasons to be angry, being able to express anger correctly can be a powerful tool.

I have not always responded in the right way when I got angry. Immersed in brokenness, I allowed worldly ways to influence how I responded. I blew up, got irritated, complained, gossiped, held grudges, crossed people out, got revenge, judged, criticized, and even fought. I allowed the wrong thing to cause me to respond in a wrong way. I lived as though I controlled the world and believed I had the right to judge people around me.

Thankfully, I am not the one in charge, God is.

> *"There is one lawgiver, who is able to save and to destroy: who art thou that judgest another?" (James 4:12).*

When angry, we act as if we are God. We judge those who hurt us or refuse to do things our way. James tells us we are wrong to judge and criticize others. There is only one lawgiver and judge with the ability to save or destroy. Only God has the right to pass judgement.

Clearly, I had a problem. I was angry and trying to take God's place in the world. I expressed anger the wrong way. I struggled with bitterness, grumbled, yelled, and argued. I needed help!

Expressing Anger the Right Way

If it's not wise to stuff our anger or blow up, what's left to do? We can go to God for help. As we do so, we will learn how to think through angry situations and deal with our anger in such a way which helps us and others.

How does God respond when something important goes wrong? Did He get angry when the perfect world He created became contaminated with sin and filth? Yes. But He responded to His anger by sending His only son to a broken world to die on the cross. He didn't kick, scream, and drag our names through the mud. He sacrificed His son, so we could be forgiven and restored to a right relationship with Him and others.

Our anger can have a similar outcome by responding in a positive way. We can learn to say, "Now that's wrong," without ranting, raving, or gossiping about what happened or calling someone hateful names.

> *"Wherefore, my beloved brethren, let every man be swift*
> *to hear, slow to speak, slow to wrath" (James 1:19).*

I learned to control my anger by responding with patience when unexpected or bad things happened. I realized I live in a world with wrongful things, such as evil people, unfair friends, disrespectful families, unloving spouses, and abusive people. In order to survive, I had to be patient in difficult situations and relationships. Most importantly, I realized this is God's world, not my own.

We all can learn to express anger in the right way. There's a place for anger when it's expressed in love from a pure heart. For instance, abusers and those who do evil toward us should be brought to justice. They need to face the consequences of their actions. We can address the wrong done to us in a way which expresses patience, love, and kindness. Responding to anger in the right way becomes an instrument in God's hands to make this bad world better.

Sleeping with Anger

Although we can spend time and energy arguing throughout the day, a different feeling emerges when anger spills over into the intimate spaces of our bedrooms. When I am angry, I try to resolve it before bed. For I have found out, if we go to bed angry, we will still have our anger when we wake up in the morning. And that's if we ever slept. Going to bed angry affects our quality of sleep, and instead of waking up refreshed, we wake up feeling dry and stale like old sandwich bread.

I had to practice not taking my anger to bed with me. If something really bothered me, I held on to it and didn't want to turn it loose. After spending so much time stewing over nothing, I would eventually simmer down. I had to learn to put things in perspective when I got angry. I would seriously ask myself, "Is this really worth losing sleep over?" In most cases, I realized my energy would be better spent by giving God the situation and focusing on other things.

> *"Be ye angry, and sin not: let not the sun go down*
> *upon your wrath" (Eph. 4:26).*

Ephesians tells us not to let the sun go down on our anger. In other words, we can hold on to anger too long. Carrying those harsh feelings to bed is not a good idea, especially for married couples. Having your arms filled with angry feelings leaves little room for cuddling and closeness.

After years of going to bed angry and tense, I now know it's not worth giving up a peaceful night. In order to sleep well and not be angry, I pray, listen to music, release my harsh feelings, and have a good night's sleep.

Set Affections on Things Above

Anger will weary our hearts and bring us to the brink of mental and emotional breakdowns. We often give our circumstances too much power. Rather than take control of our situations, we allow our circumstances to control how we think and act.

When I struggled with anger, there were many triggers . . . people, situations, memories, personal problems, etc. I spent a lot of attention and energy trying to take back control of things in my life that were out of control. I fought a losing battle. It seemed I always had things occur which did not meet my approval. I wasted a lot of precious time focusing on trivial matters. I had to learn how to keep myself calm by not putting so much attention on small stuff, rather to focus on kingdom things and let the main thing be the main thing. Paul put it this way.

> *"If ye then be risen with Christ, seek those things which are above, where Christ sitteth on the right hand of God. Set your affection on things above, not on things on the earth" (Col. 3:1–2).*

Here, we are encouraged to "set our affection on things above." We are to put our attention on what God is doing, not on what others are doing. Focusing on others can cause feelings of outrage as people are not capable of completely satisfying us. But focusing on God has a calming effect.

> *"Thou wilt keep him in perfect peace, whose mind is stayed on thee: because he trusteth in thee" (Isa. 26:3).*

When we keep God the main thing, He keeps us calm during times of upheaval and instability. After learning this, I refused to allow my circumstances to determine my emotional well-being. For being controlled by our circumstances sets us on an emotional roller coaster. I had to free myself from the oppression of "would have, should have, and could have." In doing this, I not only found peace and comfort in the midst of turmoil, I also welcomed God's power and sovereignty into my life to help me deal with anger in a more loving and caring way.

Angry at God

Have you ever been angry with God? I have. When my requests to God didn't turn out like I had hoped, I became angry, confused, and wondered if He heard me. I recall crying out to Him, expressing my disappointment and frustrations for allowing things to turn out so bad.

I know everything God does comes without fault, and He is always right. But I still think it's important for us to express our upset feelings to Him. Although He knew all about it, I still wanted to share my pain and anger. Rather than ignoring my pain by not sharing it, I wanted to confess my anger and seek God's healing.

When I became completely honest with God about how I felt, what happened next took me by surprise. God showed up! I can only describe it like a mother runs to her hurting child, God, the Father, ran to me, His child. I didn't see Him with my eyes, but I felt His touch. I knew He was with me. I felt His comfort. This encounter with God became a pivotal point in my healing. I realized God understood my flaws and feelings. He came to me when I was down and ministered comfort.

If you're angry with God, tell Him. Yes, He already knows, and He still wants you to go to Him. Lay your heart open before God. Acknowledge that, even while you don't understand what's happened, you trust He can make everything work out. It took me a while to see how my circumstances could be used for my good. God may have not granted all of my requests, but I developed a closer relationship with Him. A few years later, He turned everything around. God also healed my heart from the pain of loss and the scars left by my anger.

7

The Process of Forgiveness

When injured, our natural reaction or impulse is to protect ourselves. Forgiveness is normally not the first thing to enter our minds. We just don't naturally flow with mercy and forgiveness when we have been wronged. The results of unforgiveness can be seen everywhere. Family members don't speak to each other, homes are torn apart, and churches split. All these things happen because someone digs in their heels and refuses to let go.

Forgiveness says we have decided to release feelings of resentment toward someone who has harmed us. It's deciding to wipe the slate clean. Some of us have been betrayed and mistreated in extremely harsh ways. We have embedded wounds. But the Lord knows our pain. He knows what we have endured, and He wants to heal us. By nature, we want to hold on to the negative feelings and replay the hurtful feelings in our minds. But God has provided a way for us to regain control of our lives. He wants us to forgive and to get rid of those bad thoughts. Forgiveness paves the way by which God can bring about our healing.

> *"Then came Peter to him, and said, Lord, how oft shall my brother sin against me, and I forgive him? Till seven times? Jesus saith unto him, I say not*

unto thee, until seven times: but, until seventy times
seven" (Matt. 18:21–22).

In this Scripture, Peter thought seven would be a perfect number to forgive someone. But Jesus said we should forgive and keep forgiving. Initially, I was afraid to forgive, thinking I may get hurt again. Then I realized I may get hurt again if I chose to keep living. This is why God said to forgive "seventy times seven." There's no limit placed on the amount of times we have to forgive someone. Now I refuse to live in fear and be afraid to forgive, thinking I might get hurt again.

Forgiving can be difficult but rewarding. Forgiving others allows us to enjoy life and have more peace. But those of us who refuse to forgive will live with confusion and turmoil. We are expected to be generous in our willingness to forgive to the point we lose count of how many times we have forgiven someone.

Collecting Debts

Are you trying to collect a debt from your offender or from someone who has hurt you? This is an appropriate question to ask since many hurt people seek payment for their pain and sorrows. We feel as though someone took something that belonged to us, and now they "owe us."

Collecting debt from someone who has hurt us is aimless. I wanted the people to pay for hurting me. But what hurt would be too large for me to forgive when compared to what the Lord had forgiven me for? When I look back, I see my selfishness. My unwillingness to forgive others demonstrated my ungratefulness for what the Lord had done for me. Besides, people who hurt us are in no position to pay us back even if they wanted to.

> *But the same servant went out, and found one of*
> *his fellow servants, which owed him an hundred*
> *pence: and he laid hands on him, and took him*
> *by the throat, saying, Pay me that thou owest.*
> *And his fellow servant fell down at his feet, and*

besought him, saying, Have patience with me,
and I will pay thee all. And he would not: but
went and cast him into prison, till he should pay
the debt. (Matt. 18:28–30).

Unforgiveness involves collecting debts, but forgiveness is all about cancelling debts. The above Scripture tells us the servant was unable to pay his debt. In the same manner, our offenders don't have the ability to repay us for their offenses. No matter how much time you devote to them or what they do for you, they can't pay you back and undo the pain.

Forgiveness demonstrates God's love in action. Unforgiveness contributes to a hard heart, which magnifies the pain. When we look at unforgiveness this way, forgiveness gives us a win-win option ending with no more debt, anger, or pain.

"For we know him that hath said, Vengeance belongeth
unto me, I will recompense, saith the Lord. And again,
The Lord shall judge his people" (Heb. 10:30).

Hebrews says vengeance belongs to God, and He will settle the cases of His people, as well as repay them. Can you believe it? My mind can hardly comprehend God's mercy. But if the Bible says He will do it, I have learned to open my heart to receive it. Now I will let God pay me for past injustices and not try to collect from the people who have hurt me. I have also forgiven myself for past sins and hurts I have caused others. I can't pay people back, so I asked God to do it.

Forgive from the Heart

For years I didn't forgive, waiting to feel better. But forgiveness never took place because I never felt like doing it. Forgiveness is not a feeling, rather a choice we make with our hearts. Forgiveness emerges out of obedience to God. When someone hurts us, we may not be ready to let go of our negative feelings. In order to heal, however, we must trust God, and in faith, forgive our offenders in spite of our feelings.

For many years, I thought, "I will forgive them, but I don't want anything else to do with them." This is not true forgiveness in God's eyes. What if God told us He would forgive us, but He does not want anything else to do with us? Sounds devastating, doesn't it? God desires for us to model Christ, which means forgiving those who hurt us.

> *"So likewise, shall my heavenly Father do also unto you, if ye from your hearts forgive not everyone his brother their trespasses" (Matt. 18:35).*

According to Scripture, forgiveness must come from our hearts, not just out of our mouths. Unforgiveness breeds in our hearts and develops deep-rooted wounds that trigger our thoughts and emotions. Forgiving from the heart releases God's power over the situation and allows us to heal.

The Poison of Unforgiveness

Many people ruin their health by harboring unforgiveness. I know, because unforgiveness almost got the best of me. When someone hurt me, I tried hard to pay them back by getting revenge. I found myself playing God and deciding their fate. By judging them and taking action, I made myself feel better for a little bit. But over time, I noticed the more I did these bad things and harbored unforgiveness, the worst I felt. My heart ached; my prayers went unanswered. My life was miserable, and I didn't understand why I felt this way.

> *Therefore is the kingdom of heaven likened unto a certain king, which would take account of his servants. And when he had begun to reckon, one was brought unto him, which owed him ten thousand talents. But forasmuch as he had not to pay, his lord commanded him to be sold, and his wife,*

and children, and all that he had, and payment to be made. The servant therefore fell down, and worshipped him, saying, Lord, have patience with me, and I will pay thee all. Then the lord of that servant was moved with compassion, and loosed him, and forgave him the debt. But the same servant went out, and found one of his fellow servants, which owed him an hundred pence: and he laid hands on him, and took him by the throat, saying, Pay me that thou owest. And his fellow servant fell down at his feet, and besought him, saying, have patience with me, and I will pay thee all. And he would not: but went and cast him into prison, till he should pay the debt. So when his fellow servants saw what was done, they were very sorry, and came and told unto their lord all that was done. Then his lord, after that he had called him, said unto him, O thou wicked servant, I forgave thee all that debt, because thou desiredst me: Shouldest not thou also have had compassion on thy fellow servant, even as I had pity on thee? And his lord was wroth, and delivered him to the tormentors, till he should pay all that was due unto him. (Matt. 18:23–34).

Matthew tells us if we do not forgive people, we get turned over to the tormentors. I can bear witness to what Matthew says. Having hateful thoughts toward another person fuels bitterness.

When I allowed myself to forgive someone, initially I thought, I did it for them. I soon realized I helped myself more. When Jesus told us to forgive those who have wronged us, He was actually looking out for our best interests. Until we forgive others, we dwell on disturbing thoughts about them. As a result, we relive our past pain, which makes it difficult to get on with the rest of our lives. But when we forgive, our painful sores begin to heal. Once we pray and surrender our pains to God, He delivers us.

Previously, I looked at forgiving others as a really hard thing to do. I thought it seemed so unfair for them to receive forgiveness when I had gotten hurt. I got the pain, and they didn't even have to pay for causing it. Now I know I am helping myself when I choose to forgive.

Forgiveness in a Marriage

Being able to forgive and let go of past hurts plays a major role in a healthy marriage. If spouses hold on to every petty annoyance, hurt, and disappointment, precious time and energy may waste away. Also, nursing perceived hurts can eventually turn into something much worse, such as hate.

You may really resent your spouse for things such as being rude and forgetful, or causing major financial issues where you declare bankruptcy and possibly lose your house or vehicle. Lack of forgiveness disintegrates a marriage, affecting both spouses mentally and physically. Over time, resentment gains momentum and chips away at your relationship's foundation.

I know it may be challenging to forgive your spouse when he causes pain. During these times, you may be tempted to speak unkind things or try to get even. Instead, try releasing him from that bondage, forgive, and allow God to take over your marriage. Let Him deal with all his words, actions, and behaviors. God places high value on the sanctity of marriage. If we allow Him to take the lead, our marriages can heal despite past situations.

Forgiving a Parent

Forgiving a parent leads to unloading past baggage and allowing room for God to use those hurts in a positive way. When we have been deeply wounded by a parent and fail to let it go, our lives erode on many levels.

I had a strained relationship with my father for the majority of my life. For some reason, we always seemed to be on a different page.

This may have been due to both of us having such an outspoken personality and competitive spirit. We both had to have the last word. Plus, I wanted my father to change and do better in life, without ever realizing I needed to change too.

After spending precious years trying to change him, I finally gave up. I decided if I wanted to be happy, I would just have to let him be. Though I went on with my life, I still wasn't happy. Years went by, and my father and I were mostly on speaking terms, although meaningful communication rarely occurred between us. At the same time, all of my close relationships mirrored my relationship with him, unfruitful at best.

As time went on, I established a closer relationship with the Lord, and it wasn't long before God started to deal with my unforgiveness and my distant relationship with my earthly father. I still remember God insisting I ask my father for forgiveness. He assured me I would be held responsible if it didn't take place because I knew better.

All that time I had waited on him to apologize. But we don't need an apology from someone in order to obtain forgiveness. God said forgive even if the other person does not make an effort. Jesus shed more light on why I needed to forgive my father.

> *"Then said Jesus, Father, forgive them; for they know not what they do..." (Luke 23:34).*

Jesus forgave the people who hurt Him and even said they didn't know what they were doing. My father didn't realize the impact of his behavior. He would not have wanted me to go through a bad childhood which could have a long-lasting effect on me. If he had known how he impacted me, he would not have done those things. God gave me the grace to forgive those who hurt and wounded me, but I still struggled with forgiving my father. As I wrestled with forgiving him, I meditated on the following Scripture.

> *"Honour thy father and thy mother, as the LORD thy God hath commanded thee; that thy days may be prolonged, and that it may go well with thee, in the land which the LORD thy God giveth thee" (Deut. 5:16).*

While meditating on this Scripture, God gave me revelation of why I struggled with forgiving him so much. You see, Satan had planted seeds of doubt and deception in my mind to make me think I didn't have to forgive my father. But according to Scripture, God commanded I honor him. This commandment also has a blessing connected to it.

There's something important about the relationship of a child and her parents. God says if we honor our parents, He will bless us, and if we choose not to honor them, our lives will not go well. The choice is ours to make.

My father had not always been there for me, but he was still my father, and I couldn't change that. I finally made a decision to honor and forgive him, not for what he did to me but for who he was, my father.

8

When Words Hurt

"Sticks and stones may break my bones, but words will never hurt me." I shouted this as a child playing on the school playground. As I grew older, I found out quite the opposite: words do hurt. In fact, broken bones can heal a whole lot faster than hurtful words spoken over us. A stick or a stone may bruise our bodies for a while, but a cruel word can inflict such a wound that it lingers for years. Sticks and stones may break our bones, but hurtful words can break our hearts. I compare hurtful words to feathers. They are easy to scatter, but not easy to gather.

As a child, I allowed words to go in one ear and out the other for the most part. Later on, my feelings toward what was said to me became more personal and real. I experienced times when I thought the wounds caused by cutting words would never heal.

How can some simple words cause so many problems? How can our tongues be powerful enough to hold life and death? God's words have a purpose, and they will accomplish something. Shouldn't this also apply to us since we are made in His image?

> *"Death and life are in the power of the tongue: and they that love it shall eat the fruit thereof" (Prov. 18:21).*

"So shall my word be that goeth forth out of my mouth: it shall not return unto me void, but it shall accomplish that which I please, and it shall prosper in the thing whereto I sent it" (Isa. 55:11).

Our words carry power, and that's why they can cause problems and hindrances in our lives. We can use our words for both good and evil. Even though our tongues are a small part of our bodies, they have the power to make a tremendous impact. The words we use to communicate with one another can cut like a scalpel. In the hands of a skilled surgeon, a scalpel can do a lot of good. But in the hands of a careless person, it can cause a great deal of harm.

We can cause a lot of pain with our words, using hurtful ones to attack, control, or to hurt someone. We often overlook the great harm the tongue can inflict. It only takes a few minutes and one unkind word to injure a spouse, friend, or even a stranger.

Word Curses

Today we think of "cursing" as foul language or profanity. While true, a curse spoken over someone can cause evil to come upon them. In essence, our words can speak curses upon ourselves and those who cross our paths.

I have harmed myself numerous times through self-imposed curses. By using such negative statements as "I am so broke," "Things never work out for me," "They always pass me at promotion time," etc., I brought curses upon myself. Curses harm us because they hold us back from arriving at our divine appointments. When we speak curses over ourselves, we act against the will and purpose of God for our lives.

I often derailed opportunities because of words I spoke over myself. I didn't realize what harm I caused. My negative comments opened the door for delayed progress or worse yet, for something bad to happen. Now I am more careful about what I say. I have put down the bat and no longer use negative words to beat myself up.

Curses can also come into our lives from negative words spoken by others. The words of those in authority carry much weight, for we generally look up to them as role models. They can be parents, teachers, employees, church leaders, or those we admire. When a person in authority tells a child such harmful things as they are no good, fat, ugly, will amount to nothing, or will never make it, and if that child believes what she hears, the seeds of low self-worth are planted.

These things can lodge into our hearts and remain there for a long time. When I prepared for nursing school, I was informed by several individuals that I may not be selected, it was difficult to get in, and we didn't have any nurses from where I came from. The words spoken by them were hurtful, for they didn't believe in me.

In spite of their mean remarks, I released any harsh feelings I had toward them. I went on with God's endorsement, for God believed in me. And with His support, it was difficult to be downhearted by some unkind words.

Silence the Slander

Nothing can be more painful than when someone says something blatantly untrue about us. Known as slander, false statements can cause people to have a bad opinion about someone. In fact, few things have the power to ruin a relationship like accusing, hostile, and slanderous words.

Slander is meant to harm one's reputation or to accuse. In fact, it comes from the word *devil* derived from the Greek diablos, which means slanderer. Pure evil indeed!

> *And I heard a loud voice saying in heaven, now is come salvation, and strength, and the kingdom of our God, and the power of his Christ: for the accuser of our brethren is cast down, which accused them before our God day and night. (Rev. 12:10).*

The Bible calls Satan the accuser of the brethren. So, when people slander, they act like an evil person, intending only to harm.

It never feels good to be slandered. When I experienced it, I didn't want to appear weak, so I struck back. Immediately I tried clearing my name and aimlessly strived to set the record straight. But truthfully, most people who slander do not like us, so there's no need to try defending ourselves.

Eventually, I learned to endure it and to humble myself rather than retaliate. God showed me vindication was His job. When I surrendered my right to retaliate over to the Lord, He protected and vindicated me when needed. For He will make the wrong things right in His timing and in His own way.

Now I strive to keep my heart pure with those who mistreat me through slanderous speech. The pain from the sting of slander goes away quicker if we speak the truth in love without being defensive and refuse to retaliate, no matter what.

Telling Lies

Everyone has been affected one way or the other by lies. A destructive practice, lying has become a major issue in our society today as morals and values spiral downward. Most of us are not surprised when an enemy lies, but what about when a family member lies? Families built on trust and honesty produce healthy relationships.

Jacob's family in the Bible shows us how lies can cause problems in a family.

> *And Jacob served seven years for Rachel; and they seemed unto him but a few days, for the love he had for her. And Jacob said unto Laban, Give me my wife, for my days are fulfilled, that I may go in unto her. And Laban gathered together all the men of the place and made a feast. And it came to pass in the evening, that he took Leah his daughter, and brought her to him; and he went in unto her.*

And Laban gave unto his daughter Leah Zilpah his maid for an handmaid. And it came to pass, that in the morning, behold, it was Leah: and he said to Laban, what is this thou hast done unto me? Did not I serve with thee for Rachel? Wherefore then hast thou beguiled me? (Gen. 29:20–25).

After promising to give Rachel as a wife to Jacob, Laban, instead, gave him Leah. As a result, Jacob worked seven years for a woman he did not want to marry. Later, Jacob became so alienated and isolated that he left his father-in-law, who kept deceiving him. Eventually, both sisters married Jacob, which resulted in strife and alienation the rest of their lives. Lying creates barriers in relationships because it violates trust. Without trust, relationships can't survive.

On a personal level, lies have made me feel disrespected and unimportant. I've always felt if someone lied to me, they didn't care enough about me to tell the truth. When I feel like I know someone, I give them a big part of my heart. If they are untruthful, I know they held theirs back. Being lied to makes me feel dumb. Plus, I can't help but wonder why I received such poor treatment.

Truth of the matter, lying can't be justified, and we can still depend on God. His nature never changes. Let's observe what the Bible has to say about God's honesty and reliability.

"God is not a man that he should lie; neither the son of man that he should repent: hath he said, and shall he not do it? Or hath he spoken, and shall he not make it good?" (Num. 23:19).

In his letter to Titus, Paul stated boldly that God cannot lie. Unlike people, we can depend on God when He tells us He's going to do something. In Scripture, God mentions thousands of blessings. He has promised to bless us; therefore when trials and problems arise, we can depend on God to come through for us. He has never gone back on a promise.

Verbal Abuse

Being constantly exposed to verbal abuse can have harmful effects. Sometimes difficult to spot, verbal abuse attacks a person's character. Verbal abuse comes in many forms such as angry outbursts, sarcasm, undermining, threatening, name calling, and constant put downs. Some people may not think verbal abuse causes ill effects, but those who have been on the receiving end know its demeaning power.

For many years, verbal abuse clouded my world and sense of reality. Since most abusers are different in public than in private, the person being belittled eventually begins to feel her abuser is right and the problem lies within herself. It made me feel like something was wrong with me as I constantly struggled with my own feelings and abilities. When my feelings were consistently ignored, I began to second guess myself and became unable to stand up for what I believed.

After living with a situation for so long, where nothing changed no matter how hard I tried, I slowly gave up. I stopped caring and started to give up on life and lose heart. For a person who used to be so happy, outgoing, and full of energy, I had become sad, lethargic, and depressed. When people turned out to be completely different from what they pretended to be, feelings of betrayal set in and weighed heavy on my heart.

What affected my heart eventually brought a strain on my body. I started to experience a host of physical symptoms, such as migraines and abdominal pain. My body spoke back to me for exposing it to chronic stressful conditions. These symptoms prevented me from enjoying life. There's no question about the seriousness of the effects violent, abusive words have on their prey.

Now when the words of others hurt me, I find healing in the true Words of God. When we hurt others with our words, we can also find forgiveness in God and seek it from those we have harmed. Those who have been victims of serious verbal abuse may need the help of a counselor or pastor throughout the healing process.

God desires only healthy relationships for us, not verbally abusive ones. Angry and critical words destroy confidence and self-esteem. Being submissive in a marriage relationship does not mean allowing yourself to be verbally beaten by your spouse.

"So encourage each other and build each other up,
just as you are already doing" (1 Thess. 5:11, NLT).

Clearly, this Scripture displays God's heart on the subject of how we use our words. God wants us to encourage one another and to build each other up, not tear each other down. God longs for us to recognize the power our words carry and use them as He would.

The key to healing is to recognize the damaging effects caused by verbal abuse and to begin taking deliberate steps to stop it. Since the abuser usually carries a great deal of denial, the responsibility for recognizing verbal abuse often rests with the person being abused. Identifying the abuse and realizing it stemmed from the abuser's issues and not yours is a significant first step toward healing and restoration.

9

How I Escaped the Effects of Alcohol

Alcoholism can have a lasting impact on children. Most people underestimate the effects of being raised in an alcoholic family. Growing up in a family with a parent who has an alcohol problem can be so painful the adult child can still suffer negative consequences years later. The emotional scars inflicted by parental alcoholism can lead to dysfunctional relationships, low self-esteem, depression, anxiety, and addictive behaviors. Alcoholism isn't an individual problem, it's a systemic problem, and the ones who hurt the most don't even drink.

My father drank excessively for as long as I can remember. As a daughter of an alcoholic, I felt different and disconnected. I sensed something was wrong but didn't know what. Although relieved to discover some of my struggles common among adult children of alcoholics (ACOAs), I wanted to escape the effects of this debilitating lifestyle. I purposely sought the Lord, in an effort to better understand myself and to find out how to keep alcohol from ruining my life.

> *"There hath no temptation taken you but such as is common to man: but God is faithful, who will not suffer you to be tempted above that ye are able; but will with the temptation also make a way to escape, that ye may be able to bear it" (1 Cor. 10:13).*

Yes, I had come from an alcoholic family, but I didn't have to let it destroy me. God made a way for me to escape its grip and get out from under the heavy load. Because of His healing power and the path He led me down to recover from having an alcoholic father, I no longer live in isolation and silence, but freedom.

Childhood Memories

Some people can't remember much about their childhoods. However, others can't forget it. I have vivid memories of growing up and can remember past events as if they happened yesterday. As I reflect on my upbringing, I experience mixed emotions. Frequently, I received mixed messages like "Deny what you see" or "I love you but go away." My childhood experiences exposed me to both good and bad behaviors. I remember how my father behaved when drinking or how he could be verbally abusive. Yet this same man told me how smart I was and often bragged about me to others. The split personality inflicted pain daily. I hated alcoholism, but I loved my father.

The negative experiences of alcoholism led me to encounter fears and concerns. I often felt disappointed by broken promises and the inconsistent behavior which occurred more frequent than not. I was also afraid of the violence and the possibility of my parents being injured. I worried a lot about them. Frequently I cried at my parents' inappropriate behavior, which included arguments and fights. The arguing and fighting between them troubled me more than the alcoholic drinking.

Alcoholism has many victims, but perhaps the most defenseless are children of alcoholics. I didn't really understand addictions as a child, so I blamed myself and felt crazy because my experiences didn't line up with what people told me. I often heard, "Everything is fine," but my young mind knew better. Denying and ignoring true feelings defined our norm. Sometimes I struggled to express myself, remembering what punishment might occur.

Chaos defined my environment, and my stress level blew the top off the scale. I spent a lot of time alone in my room wishing I were somewhere else.

In Control

Feeling out of control scares most people, but especially ACOAs. Living with an alcoholic makes life scary and unpredictable, especially as a child. Trying to control people and situations is a coping strategy ACOAs use to deal with their dysfunctional home environments. From an early age, I tried to get my dad to stop drinking and behaving in embarrassing ways. At times, I tried controlling him; at others, I felt completely powerless. Trying to control people and situations gave me a sense of power and a sense I wouldn't be victimized anymore. I felt safe when in control and became terrified that scary and horrific things would happen if I weren't.

All this stress created fear, which fueled me to control people and situations even more. I seemed to have an unrelenting need to orchestrate everything and everyone in my life. Things had to be my way, or I would emotionally unravel and find it hard to cope. I would get visibly upset when things didn't turn out the way I wanted. Not being in control made me feel vulnerable.

These controlling behaviors caused me so much stress and other problems. I felt I had to know everything, be perfect, and know what to do all the time. At the heart of my control issues was difficulty trusting others. Adults are not always reliable in alcoholic families, and children end up emotionally neglected. When children can't trust their parents, they respond with an intense need to control things themselves.

In denial of my own feelings, I had a hard time with transitions and change. I needed routine and predictability which helped me feel safe. Rigid and inflexible, a sudden change of plans triggered my anxiety.

Regardless of all my striving for control, I ended up feeling completely powerless and out of control. I had to surrender and allow things to happen naturally. I stopped trying to get people to do what I wanted. Now I accept things will not always go the way I'd like, but I can still cope.

> *"Not that I speak in respect of want: for I have learned, in whatsoever state I am, therewith to be content" (Phil. 4:11).*

The Bible clearly teaches us to be content in whatever we face. Thanks to this Scripture's encouragement, no matter my circumstances, now I can trust God and be satisfied. I don't have to control the situation because I can depend on God, knowing His will is perfect. I can be content and remain calm and flexible. Instead of using energy to control things, I use it to enjoy things.

Keeping Secrets

Having and keeping secrets can be an exciting part of childhood. They build trust and bond people together. It can be fun to know only you and someone else share a secret. Some people remain my best friends today because we shared secrets when we were young.

On the negative side, however, some secrets cause significant pain. Alcoholism seemed like a dirty secret, so I often felt I couldn't talk about my home life. Unlike the positive side of secrets which can bind you with others, the negative isolates you.

My family didn't talk much about alcoholism or confront it. As a result, I buried my feelings and ignored my own needs. I grew up feeling out of place and isolated myself. I didn't feel, talk, or trust.

Alcoholism inflicted a tremendous amount of pain and suffering on my family. Everyone who spent time at my home witnessed and even experienced the trauma it caused. Deep down, I knew keeping everything a secret could not be in my family's best interest, as it was a toxic brew, emotionally damaging to everyone involved.

Overcoming the negative effects of my father's alcoholism took a long time due to the denial. I got so frustrated at times. I didn't understand how we could keep denying something so evident and harmful. In addition to the alcohol, the denial became a major family secret too. Reluctantly I went along with it, in an attempt to hold our family together.

> *"He that covereth his sins shall not prosper: but whoso confesseth and forsaketh them shall have mercy" (Prov. 28:13).*

When dealing with sin, there's a choice to make. We can hide it from others and go on sinning or confess it and allow God to heal us. Although drinking in and of itself does not qualify as a sin, the damage inflicted upon others from excessive drinking is unacceptable. Alcoholism puts people in bondage, not just those drinking, but others around them as well. When I pleaded to God for help, He came and rescued me. I painfully took the muzzle off my mouth and let the secrets out. This choice greatly affected my life.

Carrying Childhood into Adulthood

Growing up in an alcoholic family had a profound impact on me. I developed a lot of childhood patterns which helped me adjust as best as I could. But we don't outgrow the effects of an alcoholic family when we leave home. Even as an adult, I still use some of the same unhealthy patterns when I interact with others. Though no longer in the same house, I couldn't separate the past from the present and carried my childhood trauma into adulthood.

Many behaviors I used as a child helped me survive in a chaotic environment. While some of these have helped me with relationships, others have created more problems than not. Being aggressive and in control empowered me as a child but served as barriers later on in life.

As I began healing emotionally, I realized the unhealthy behaviors had become enmeshed in my world. In order to break free from these habits, I had to painfully dig deep inside myself. I examined which parts of those behaviors were worth keeping and which ones needed to go. Though difficult, I gradually broke away from my childhood trauma and fully embraced my life as an adult.

Learning to Relax

Children of alcoholics believe the world is a very serious place. We view life as difficult and almost always painful. Such belief develops a negative thinking pattern and self-image of being ugly, unlovable, stupid, and wrong. We work twice as hard as anyone else just to feel okay. Emotionally on guard, we stay prepared for any situation that may arise.

When I was young, there were times I didn't feel like a child. Even as I got older, I felt more mature than some of my peers. I took myself way too seriously, as well as everything I did. People who didn't take things as seriously as I did ignited frustration and contempt.

Having suffered abuse, I had to grow up early to take care of myself. My learned instincts pushed me to become a workaholic, always trying to prove my worth and make others happy. Work projects dealing with crises gave me a sense of purpose. I felt comfortable and fulfilled when I accomplished something. I didn't know how to relax, play, and enjoy life. I would labor hard all day at work and then take additional projects home. My job became a substitute for living. My identity became what I did.

I played as a child, but as I got older, I felt playing was a waste of time. After all, serious people didn't play. I felt it important to always have something to do. I thought of having fun as unproductive and not okay. It's difficult for ACOAs to have fun because so many social events and holidays get disrupted by the alcoholic parent. They don't expect to have fun.

As an adult, it felt awkward to learn to relax and enjoy life. This meant I had to risk shaking off my premature adulthood which was thrust upon me. Some years ago, I realized I had really not enjoyed very much of my thirty-plus years.

"The thief cometh not, but for to steal, and to kill,
and to destroy: I am come that they might have

96

life, and that they might have it more abundantly"
(John 10:10).

John tells us Jesus said he came to this earth, so I could have life. I had to get back to enjoying life and prevent burning myself out by being so serious all the time. I felt it essential to develop a healthy sense of humor. I worked hard, so I should play hard. I needed to laugh more and chill out. I learned to take life easy and not take myself and everything else so seriously. Work never ends. There is always something to do. Over time, I have done much better with this concept, and now I leave work to be done the next day.

Trying to be Normal

One of my childhood challenges was trying to make a choice between two options. I could adapt to the alcoholism and try to become a "good" child of an alcoholic, or I could try to have a normal childhood and have my needs met. Though I tried, doing both proved difficult.

Being a good child of an alcoholic brought challenges. To be a good child of an alcoholic meant I had to deny the alcoholism, hide my emotions, please others, and pretend to be happy. These behaviors do not produce a happy childhood, let alone a happy adult.

On the other hand, trying to have a normal childhood didn't work out for me either because I needed others' support. This was not possible as most of the people close to me remained emotionally drained and unable to continually meet my needs.

Therefore, if I tried to become a good daughter, my own needs went unmet. If I tried to be normal and to have the same experiences as children of nonalcoholic families, I quickly discovered I lacked support. Either way I looked at it, the outcomes were painful. Yet I tried to play it safe by playing both roles. Regardless of how hard I tried, I felt pain and sensed my life was out of control.

I went along guessing at what I thought normal looked like. I compare this to walking in the dark woods without a flashlight. I struggled and couldn't distinguish good role models from bad ones.

In addition, I thought everyone else was normal but me. Later on, I came to realize I acted "normal" for growing up the way I did. When children grow up in an alcoholic environment, they all feel similar things typical for their situations.

Survive Now, Heal Later

Growing up as a child, I intentionally learned how to ride a bike and hula-hoop. But I also learned some unintended lessons. I figured if I were going to have a decent childhood, I had to learn how to survive at all costs. As a result of experiencing pain, I learned how to survive in the moment. I figured I could heal later but had to survive to get there.

One of the most painful lessons I learned in my family was how to cope by developing survival skills. I learned how to withdraw, be confrontational, and act out in other ways. To avoid pain, I became a people pleaser and a manipulator. I grew up quickly with very little time to be a child. At school, I kept up a false front of normalcy while the pain of my home life drained my youthful resources. I learned how to shut down emotionally and to self-medicate my pain through pretending and living in a fantasy world.

I didn't realize I had learned all these unhealthy things. When in the middle of a crisis, we don't have time to look for help. We are too busy surviving.

As humans, we have built-in responses to danger and remarkable survival skills. When threatened, we know how to protect ourselves. In a dysfunctional family, surviving becomes a "normal" state over time.

These behaviors became natural to me since they were how I survived at an early age. While once protective and necessary, they became unhealthy for me and destructive in my adult life. Nevertheless, I struggled with giving them up because they got me through chaos.

As I worked toward healing, I realized my unhealthy survival techniques had caused me to lose sight of my inner self and reality. I knew I had to make changes but had no idea how or where to start.

How do I change my childhood liabilities into adulthood assets? These behaviors had left me powerless and spiritually bankrupt.

An Empty Love Tank

I have always heard love makes the world go round. The need to feel love is critical for human beings. Every child has an emotional tank waiting to be filled with love. Essential for emotional maturity, love and affection go a long way toward a child becoming a responsible adult. But when a child's love tank sits on empty, she will be emotionally off balance.

Growing up in an alcoholic home confused the definition of love. We talked about love, but I rarely saw it in action. Instead, I witnessed people controlling and manipulating others, making someone else's problem theirs, and losing sight of their own lives while tending to someone else's. I watched love stories on TV, and they looked nothing like what I saw. This left me trying to figure out what love really was.

All I wanted was to be loved. I spent years trying to figure it out, but I never really got a good grasp on it.

When children of alcoholics don't have their needs met at home, they grow up holding cups with holes in them. They have adult bodies, look and talk like adults, but they are little children who never got their needs met. This hole in their souls fuels their needs to be loved.

As a child, my hunger for love went unsatisfied. Deep down inside, I hurt and had a love tank with its gauge on empty. I had no love to give. This secret pain led me to look for more love in all the wrong places with the wrong people in unhealthy ways.

I felt depressed and trampled with no hope, like being sucked into a dark hole. I took my faith seriously and tried to obey God. I went to church and became addicted to the praise and worship, but there was no real change. I even poured out my pain to others but never felt any better.

Later on when I started having relationship issues, I didn't panic initially. I had been accustomed to screaming, arguing, and fighting, so I accepted the "love" I thought I deserved. But it's difficult to get love and affection from an abusive mate. And as time went by, I began to wonder why I continued to allow people to hurt me. *Do I really need this person in my life to feel good about myself? Why do I look for love in people who are incapable of loving me?*

Finally, I saw where I played a major role in perpetuating the problem. Motivated by the cravings of an empty love tank, I tolerated emotional and physical abuse for many years. I knew abuse wasn't healthy, but I had the need to feel loved. Besides, if I left, I would be at fault for messing up the relationship, although staying gave my abuser the green light to continue. I became a prisoner in my own home. Receiving love in an abusive relationship lasts only briefly. When I came down from my high of being in love, my tank registered empty again. I was forced to face a painful truth. I needed love before I could "fall in love."

> *"And hope maketh not ashamed; because the love of God is shed abroad in our hearts by the Holy Ghost which is given unto us" (Rom. 5:5).*

Paul tells us the love of God spreads abroad in our hearts by the Holy Spirit. God's love pours out to us in an unlimited supply. How deep the Father's love is for us! Now I no longer run around on empty, for God loves me beyond all measure. When I need love, I go to Him. He keeps my love tank full.

10

When the Vow Breaks

Marriage vows are meant to be permanent, although many end in divorce. A divorce can be heartbreaking, nerve-wracking, and exhausting. A major life change, divorce qualifies as one of the few times people can make changes to health insurance.

By the grace of God, I have survived two divorces. It took years for me to recover. Regardless of the circumstances surrounding the situation, divorce leaves devastation in its path.

How God Feels about Divorce

Our society has a lot to say about divorce, who's right, who's wrong, and who gets the house or custody of the kids. Everybody has an opinion. But it would be wise for us to first take a moment to see what the Bible says about marriage, so we can understand fully how God feels about divorce.

> *"Therefore shall a man leave his father and his mother, and shall cleave unto his wife: and they shall be one flesh" (Gen. 2:24).*

When God created marriage, He created it to be a perfect picture of unity between a man and a woman. Marriage is a covenant, not just a commitment. When two people choose to break that vow, it damages the picture of God's covenant with us. So marriage originated as God's idea, His plan. Now let's see how God feels about divorce.

> *"'For I hate divorce!' says the* LORD, *the God of Israel. 'To divorce your wife is to overwhelm her with cruelty,' says the* LORD *of Heaven's Armies . . ."* *(Mal. 2: 16, NLT).*

This verse tells us exactly how God feels about divorce. He hates it! God hates divorce because it deviates from His original plan. Divorce goes against God's covenant between man and woman. God never intended for divorce to be a part of our experiences, and it displeases Him when we break the vow He created. Now hate is strong language, but when we look at what divorce does and the negative impact it has on everyone involved, we will understand why God used such strong language of "hate."

I can't adequately describe my feelings after going through a divorce. It turned my world upside down and triggered all sorts of hurts and painful emotions, too deep to talk about. Divorce left me feeling devastated, confused, and ashamed. But even though God hates divorce, He loves divorced people and families. He wants us healed and made whole again.

Why Divorce Is Painful

I had not put a lot of thought into the emotional pain divorce causes until I went through my own. I had this belief of a couple coming to a mutual agreement to divorce, and they went their separate ways. Then my own divorce came with intense emotional pain and pressure. It took years for me and my family to heal. Having a personal experience changes how we look at things.

A divorce inflicts pain on many fronts. First of all, when two people make a covenant in a marriage, they become one. So, when I got divorced, my heart broke. I felt as if someone had taken away something which was once a vital part of me and now I had to make major adjustments in life without it. This pain can be similar to the loss of a loved one to death.

A divorce is painful due to the death of the marriage, but it also speaks of death to dreams and hopes. I had big dreams and had made plans of what I wanted to accomplish with my marriage. With the divorce, I realized those dreams had been washed down the drain, and I had to start over and ignite a new dream.

I experienced a lot of emotional pain accepting the fact my family would no longer be together. My pain magnified because poor innocent children were involved and caught in the crossfire. Yes, I hurt, but my children suffered the greatest loss of all, living with one parent while living apart from the other one.

Initially the pain stung so badly, I didn't want to face it. I covered up my feelings of hurt, anger, and grief. But covering up made me feel worst. I had to open up and face a painful truth. I was no longer married.

"Humble yourselves in the sight of the Lord, and he shall lift you up" (James 4:10).

A divorce is a humbling experience. Once I was able to humble myself and look the divorce straight in the face, God lifted me up. I used the pain to motivate myself to get the help I needed to heal. I knew if I could work through the recovery process, the pain would pass, and I would come out a healthier and more mature person.

Feeling like a Failure

Have you ever felt like a failure? A divorce can cause us to have those feelings. Although common in our society today, divorce still carries a certain degree of embarrassment. Feelings of being a failure can also emerge because we couldn't have a successful marriage. I had managed a lot of things and people but couldn't keep my marriage together. I felt like a failure and isolated myself from family, friends, and even the church.

"My flesh and my heart faileth: but God is the strength of my heart, and my portion forever" (Ps. 73:26).

When I turned to Scripture for answers, I read this passage from Psalms 73 and realized, though my marriage may have failed, I was not a failure. Clearly, the Bible states God lives in me, and there is no failure in God. His voice of triumph overrules every failed situation and circumstance. Instead of feeling like a failure, I learned from it. I realized the only way I could really fail would be by not trying again. Failure is never final, and the only real failure comes in not getting up again.

Healing the Pain of Divorce

Divorce betrays the vows to stick together "for better or for worse." The pain can be excruciating, and some never recover completely. We blame others and often wonder where God was when our wedding vows went up in flames. Others feel guilty, thinking God might not help them. But God stands right there ready to bring comfort to our hearts. God can and will soothe the pain. I gained healing and a measure of closure by letting go of my anger.

The pain of a second divorce left me with an even deeper sense of loss, and I didn't know how I would recover. I wondered if it would be possible for me to heal a second time around. But just when I almost came unglued, Jesus came along and comforted me. He wasn't bothered by my two divorces. I recalled the story in the Bible where Jesus met the Samaritan woman at the well.

"'I don't have a husband,' the woman replied. Jesus said, 'You're right! You don't have a husband—for you have had five husbands, and you aren't even married to the man you're living with now. You certainly spoke the truth!'" (John 4:17–18, NLT).

The Samaritan woman had gone through five ugly divorces. I can only imagine the painful scars she endured. But when she met Jesus, she confronted her failures and left the well, enthusiastic and healed.

After a divorce, many go through life changing partners, searching for something which can never be found apart from the healing a personal relationship with God can bring. Jesus is an expert at bringing healing and restoration. I recovered from the damage divorce inflicted by working at it one day at a time with God's help.

The Lord Is My Husband

After going through two divorces, I didn't want anything else to do with another marriage. I thought, maybe marriage wasn't for me. *I will just stay single and join the "singles" ministry at church.* Then God began to show me the kind of husband He could be toward me as my provider, protector, counselor, and friend. Just the thought that I could have all of these things in one man excited me!

> *"For thy Maker is thine husband; the LORD of hosts is his name; and thy Redeemer the Holy One of Israel; The God of the whole earth shall he be called" (Isa. 54:5).*

Here in Isaiah, it says the God who made me can be my spouse. This Scripture told me I had to first look to God as my husband before I could recognize a godly man. As I began to understand God's love for me, I was better able to recognize unconditional love in a man. I saw how I deserved to be treated. God filled the hole in my heart with a sense of fulfillment only He can provide. Now I am married to a godly husband. But even being married to him, I quickly learned my husband was not perfect in the ways God is. My earthly husband cannot be God in my life and meet all of my emotional needs. While he does what he can to love me in the way God has called him to, only the Lord can love me in a way which completes me and will never hurt me.

Are you still waiting for a godly man to come into your life? If so, let God be the man. He wants to be the one to "husband" you. He wants to be the one you depend on and look to first to be your provider, protector, comforter, and friend. He is the only one who's able to go to the grave and back to save you.

Divorce Recovery

Getting over a divorce can be a long and sometimes painful process. But we don't have to face it alone.

My life was pretty much in shambles after the divorce. I needed someone to talk to about my feelings and to listen to me. In an effort to make a fresh start, I began attending a different church. When I went, I expected just a good Sunday morning service but received so much more. I discovered the church had a "women's ministry" where women gathered to fellowship and support each other. I wondered if the women could be of help to me. I had always been a private person and only allowed a select few into my world. Initially, I hesitated to attend, but deep down, I knew God had prompted me. Finally, I decided to join.

Just looking at these women, I assumed they knew nothing about divorce. But at my very first meeting, I felt the connection. These women were a God-send. Genuinely concerned for me, they cared and poured their hearts into me. I was able to open up in the group and share my hurts, because I found out these women had gone through divorces and similar struggles just like me. They had grown wiser, stronger, and ready to help others.

> *"We then that are strong ought to bear the infirmities*
> *of the weak, and not to please ourselves" (Rom. 15:1).*

The women's ministry modeled Scripture. They strengthened me during my times of weakness, selflessly giving me comfort, encouragement, and a sense of strength. They prayed for me and listened without being judgmental. Some people may not understand the damaging effects of a divorce, but there are caring people, especially in churches, who understand what we are going through, and they really do want to help.

At the end of the meeting, the facilitator requested my contact information and encouraged someone to call and follow up with me. I left my phone number but didn't expect a call. Within a week, someone from the ministry had contacted me. I was shocked! I felt God had set me up. To Him, it wasn't just about the church service but also about me connecting with people who could help me recover from the divorce. The entire experience far exceeded my expectations.

Previously, I had been tempted to crawl up in a corner after the divorce. I didn't want to see or talk to anyone. But face-to-face emotional support from loving people played an essential role in my recovery. The support and love they poured into me gave me the encouragement and direction I needed for a new beginning and a hope-filled future. I am forever indebted.

11

Grieving the Loss

One of life's biggest challenges arrives when trying to cope with the loss of someone or something you love. The pain of a loss can feel overwhelming. There may be all kinds of unexpected emotions, from shock to anger, denial, guilt, and sadness.

Grief makes it difficult to do simple things, like eat, sleep, and even think. A natural response to a loss, grief is the emotional suffering we feel when something or someone we love is taken away. The more significant the loss, the more intense our grief.

Common causes of grief include relationship breakups or divorce, death of a loved one, losing a family home, or loss of a pet. Even less subtle losses can stimulate feelings of grief, such as graduating from college or moving away from home.

Whatever your loss, it's personal to you, so don't be ashamed about how you feel. If the person, animal, relationship, or situation played a significant role in your life, grieving your loss is normal and healthy. Coping with grief will help ease the pain and sadness, as well as help find the strength to move on with life.

The Death of a Parent

The death of a loved one is often the most intense type of grief and may be the deepest pain we ever experience. It can be overwhelming, frightening, and painful.

The death of a parent, in particular, has been rated the most stressful of all life-changing situations. I didn't think my father's death would hit me so hard. I was accustomed to death and dying. I even worked as a hospice nurse and witnessed death on a frequent basis. I knew death was a part of life and how to handle it in an appropriate manner. But it didn't mean I shouldn't mourn the death of my father.

When my father died, for the first time in a long time, I realized all he had done for me as a child. Before my father's death, I knew he would die someday. But understanding and anticipating did not prepare me for the grief I felt when he passed away.

Grief is the loss of a connection, and even though I had grown up and no longer lived with my dad, we were still connected. Society asserts pressure to quickly work through grief and get back on track. But how long should one grieve for a man who was your father for forty-seven years? The loss may have lasted for a moment, but, thankfully, memories last a lifetime. The grief is real, because loss is real. It doesn't matter how old we are. The death of a parent can be truly taxing. It's not easy to say goodbye.

"Jesus wept," (John 11:35).

Grieving for our loved ones is appropriate and expected. Christ Himself wept at the graveside of Lazarus. We can take heart knowing we can find comfort in more than friends and families. The very God of our creation who knows us better than we know ourselves, understands our pain and will heal us and give us peace.

Grieving with pain is all a normal part of the process. Knowing this may not minimize our grief, but it may give us courage to allow ourselves to go through the process. Only then can true healing begin.

Feeling the Emotions

The bond between a parent and a child is the deepest of all human ties. When a parent dies, the bond breaks, and we experience a multitude of strong emotions. When my father passed away on March 4, 2017, I began to feel a wave of strong emotions such as numbness and deep sadness.

When I heard the dreadful news, my feelings numbed. I felt funny all over. I guess this was my body's way of protecting me from being completely overwhelmed by the devastating news I had just received. I couldn't fully express my emotions right away. I couldn't feel anything, much less cry. I just wanted to be there for my family, especially my mom, who loved him dearly.

As the numbness wore off, I began to feel sad. After all, someone who loved me and cared for me was now gone. I expected to feel sad, but the overwhelming depth of my feelings surprised me. As I thought about my stubbornness and how I wasn't always a good daughter toward him, I experienced sorrow. My relationship with my father was rocky and distant. When he died, I felt guilty and wished we had more time together.

Finally, I was able to embrace the pain of him no longer being here, and I began to feel the hurt. I was able to cry and get it all out. An important part of my healing, I had to mourn the loss of my father in my own way. I remember sitting on the side of my bed, crying with a heavy heart.

> "Cast thy burden upon the LORD, and he shall sustain thee: he shall never suffer the righteous to be moved" (Ps. 55:22).

The pain of my father's death was too much for me to bear. I had to give it to God. I threw my pain, sorrow, and heartache upon His shoulders. God sustained me and brought me peace. Feeling all of those emotions might have felt strange, but I didn't repress them. I knew my feelings were normal and healthy, and that I had to work through them.

Not Grieving Long Enough

When grieving, we must allow ourselves to work through the various stages. One of the most common mistakes we make is to try to rush through the grieving process. We feel if we don't hurry up and snap out of it we appear weak and dysfunctional. Grieving properly, however, plays a crucial part in healing and cannot be rushed.

If we don't allow ourselves to grieve properly and instead, suppress our emotions, we can become mentally and physically off balance. Suppressing the feelings will only make the grief stronger and eventually opens the door for anger, depression, and even suicide. Deep hurts require deep healing and appropriate mourning.

Following my divorce, I grieved the loss of my marriage. I still hurt and didn't want to rush into another relationship. Plus, I needed to at least allow the ink to dry on the divorce papers! Besides, I wasn't ready for another relationship. If I moved too soon and married again without resolving the past, I was destined to repeat it.

God wants us to take time to acknowledge our feelings and take the proper time to grieve before moving on. Let's see how God guided the time of Joshua's grief when Moses died.

> *"And the children of Israel wept for Moses in the plains of Moab thirty days: so the days of weeping and mourning for Moses were ended" (Deut. 34:8).*

> *"Moses my servant is dead; now therefore arise, go over this Jordan, thou, and all this people, unto the land which I do give to them, even to the children of Israel" (Joshua 1:2).*

The children of Israel grieved the death of Moses for thirty days. Joshua had to take thirty days for grieving because there was a specific time for them to cross over into the promised land. If they had not taken the time to grieve, they would have missed their timing.

We may say thirty days doesn't seem long enough to grieve, but Joshua was led by the Lord, and he knew when his time to grieve had ended. We must allow the Lord to take our hands and lead us through the seasons of grief. We do not want to give Satan an opportunity to create a stronghold of grief in our minds, which will keep us from moving into the things God plans for us.

Grieving Too Long

Grief is important and necessary, although we can grieve too long. For example, if you lost a job three years ago and are still bitter, you need to recognize that season of your life ended and move on.

I dealt with the grief of a lost marriage for several months. Although I didn't rush the process, I also didn't want to spend the rest of my life grieving. Unfortunately, life didn't stop just because I hurt. Despite grief, I had to take care of my children, do the chores, and pay bills. I went through the grief and recovered to the point where I no longer felt weighted down by the ex-spouse and the breakup. When the pain was a distant memory, I felt I could move on.

> *"To everything there is a season, and a time to every purpose under the heaven . . . A time to weep, and a time to laugh; a time to mourn, and a time to dance" (Eccles. 3:1, 4).*

Grieving has its time and place in our lives, just like everything else. God has an appointed time for grieving, which differs for everyone. You must be in tune with Him and know His voice, so you will know when the time has come to move on.

> *"And the LORD said unto Samuel, how long wilt thou mourn for Saul, seeing I have rejected him from reigning over Israel? Fill thine horn with oil, and go, I will send thee to Jesse the Bethlehemite: for I have provided me a king among his sons" (1 Sam. 16:1).*

God's appointed time for Samuel to grieve over Saul losing his anointment as king had ended. God instructed Samuel to get up and go anoint another king. If Samuel had continued to mourn for Saul, he would have missed the next move of God through David. Staying in denial and in seasons of grief for a prolonged period robs us of our strength, the very thing we need in order to move into our next seasons with God. But we must get up and go when God says the grieving is over before we can embrace our new seasons, which are often greater than what we had before the loss.

Celebrating the Life

When a loved one dies, it's important to grieve the loss, but equally important to acknowledge his or her life. Celebrating someone's life rejoices in the fact he or she lived and allows people to reflect on how the person touched their lives. A celebration of life also helps to hasten the healing process because it helps survivors recognize the end of a loved one's life on earth, accept the loss, and make the necessary adjustments.

Memories can be funny, happy or sad, but they all tell a story. It's important for us to share those memories because they bring meaning to our lives and to the life of the person who died. Initially, memories may be too painful to recall, but if you reach through the pain and allow your mind to reflect, memories can be a comfort.

My father had a very special life made up of his beliefs, dreams, struggles, and the things he loved which brought him joy. Instead of focusing on the undesirable aspects of my father's life, I chose to concentrate on the positive things and the precious memories. I also found it calming and reassuring to keep a physical reminder of my father. I have his red scarf and beautiful candelabra from his room. I love scarves and candles. These items serve not only as personal treasures, but as tangible proof of my father's individuality and attachments. These items give me a vibrant memory and comfort when grief overtakes me.

After his death, we held a public memorial to celebrate his life. Our family wore his favorite color, red. What a joyous day! Although some sadness fell upon the room, overall, it was a day of celebration. As I sat in the service listening to the music and the individual remarks about my father, my pain diminished, and I had a sense of peace. Mourning his passing helped to bring closure and comfort.

> *"Blessed are they that mourn: for they shall be comforted" (Matt. 5:4).*

This Scripture has been a source of strength during my times of loss. Jesus blesses us when we are grief-stricken and mourn. He comforts those who are broken-hearted and filled with deep sadness. It's comforting to know when I experience deep sadness, God is real.

If you have lost someone dear to you, be comforted by celebrating his or her life and embrace God's grace and love. For He embraces all mourning, whatever loss we face. He will comfort, strengthen, and keep us.

12

Dealing with Depression

A leading problem which affects millions today, depression can be described as the common cold of our emotions. It can affect anyone as no one is immune to it. Depression inflicts a heavy emotional fog which stubbornly clouds our hopes and happiness. It leaves us with feelings of sadness, fatigue, and anger. Depressed people can feel worthless, become suicidal, and lose interest in things they once enjoyed. Horrible life circumstances such as loss of employment, divorce, abuse, and trauma trigger depression.

More than a temporary feeling of sadness which we all have from time to time, depression is real. It looms over us like a dark cloud, dragging us down. We feel weak and dry, crumbling under the weight.

I think back on my depressive days and I remember those feelings of deep sadness and loneliness. Those feelings of depression came in when I felt emotionally and mentally drained because the pain was so great. I had struggled so long with the pain until it eventually weighed me down. I didn't want to see or talk to anyone. I just wanted to be left alone. Some days, I could hardly muster up enough strength to get out of bed.

Hurting people easily shut off from others because they fear being hurt again. When hurting, we feel all people are bad, and no one can help us. To "take some control," we isolate ourselves by staying locked in a room, getting under the covers, sitting in the dark, or turning our faces to the wall. But this doesn't help, it only makes us feel worst. So what can we do to help us feel better?

> *"Create in me a clean heart, O God; and renew*
> *a right spirit within me. Cast me not away from*
> *thy presence; and take not thy holy spirit from me.*
> *Restore unto me the joy of thy salvation; and uphold*
> *me with thy free spirit" (Ps. 51:10–12).*

When depressed and feeling low, we can do like King David did. He prayed when his heart felt heavy for committing adultery and disobeying God's commandments. He could have gone somewhere and buried his head in the sand, but he didn't. Instead, he prayed for God to renew his spirit and to restore his joy.

When life leaves us dry, weak, and depleted, we can go to God. He will help us and hold us up with His right hand.

Taking Time to Rest

When we are weak, our bodies become tired. We also become easily frustrated. This makes us vulnerable to feeling discouraged and burned out. When discouraged, we are prone to depression. During these moments we have to slow down, rest, and not push our bodies past our limits.

Fatigue contributed to my depression. After working eight to ten hours a day, I would dart to different places without taking care of my own needs. Finally, at night I would fall into bed, get about six hours of sleep, only to wake up the next day and do the same routine again. Although I slept, I became exhausted because I lacked rest. Vital to our mental well-being, rest is required for us to properly function and survive. When I look at the story of Elijah and his bouts of depression, I notice Elijah was tired and needed to rest.

> *But he himself went a day's journey into the*
> *wilderness and came and sat down under a juniper*

tree: and he requested for himself that he might die; and said, it is enough; now, O LORD, take away my life; for I am not better than my fathers. And as he lay and slept under a juniper tree, behold, then an angel touched him, and said unto him, arise and eat. (1 Kings 19:4–5).

Elijah was physically exhausted and emotionally empty. What happened to the mighty man of God? In the previous chapters, we saw Elijah call down fire from heaven and defeat more than four hundred prophets of Baal, as well as outrun a chariot. Now in this Scripture above, he runs from Jezebel who threatens to kill him. As he sits under a juniper tree and wants to die, he falls asleep.

Just like Elijah, when we are tired, our emotions can dwindle and cause us to fall apart. This isn't the time for us to go above and beyond by trying to prove how strong we are. We can't run at record-breaking pace. We have to slow down, rest, and allow God to strengthen us.

Arise

While we need rest in order to be strengthened, we also have to maintain balance in life. While resting, we can't allow depression to sneak up on us and zap our energy. We can become so drained until all we want to do is lie down and take a nap. But if we are going to come out of depression, we can only do so by standing up, not lying down. We must get up and get going or life will pass us by.

When I battled depression, I slept way too much. I had to get out of bed and stop feeling sorry for myself. Constantly overwhelmed with feelings of despair, I had to arise, get on my feet, and shake myself from all the lethargy and hopelessness. The time had come for me to get back in the race. Yes, it was easy to just lie around and do nothing, but I had been in the valley long enough.

*"And the angel of the LORD came again the second time,
and touched him, and said, Arise and eat; because the
journey is too great for thee" (1 Kings 19:7).*

Depression is all about elevation. Once on the mountain top, Elijah now sat in the dumps, seeing things from the bottom up. At a lower place than he was supposed to be, the angel told him to arise and leave the lower level of his life.

God intends a much higher place for us. With each new season, God elevates many who are willing to get up off the ground and leave depression behind. He quickens those who have become ill, weary, and burdened. This involves putting down the old way of doing things. He wants to set our hearts on higher things, which are above the lower life of this fallen world.

Food for the Journey

If you battle depression, what do you feed yourself? TV, social media, and worldly news? While these things may satisfy fleshly appetites, they feed depression.

If we feel bad physically, we have to stop eating junk food. Emotionally, depression works the same way. If we want to feel better, we must allow God to feed us. We need His food, because life is a journey, and we can't survive living off stuff with no lasting value. When God feeds us, we can go further than we ever thought possible.

I remember when I was stubborn and depressed. I refused to accept the people God sent to help me. I continued to pout and stew under my own juniper tree. God sent friends and ministers to comfort me, but I resisted them. Too stubborn to listen, I didn't realize God was busy on my behalf bringing me the food I needed to survive. I had to stop being stubborn to allow God to help me.

God sends His angels to minister comfort when we hurt and need strength. When Elijah was afraid and running for his life, an angel appeared to him and provided food and water for his journey.

"And he arose, and did eat and drink, and went in the strength of that meat forty days and forty nights unto Horeb the mount of God" (1 Kings 19:8).

When going through tough times, we sometimes focus on our lack and see only that we have no time or money. But God has already provided help for us. Why do we have to eat when we feel down? Because the journey is too great for us. We won't make it without God refueling us. In the midst of our troubles, He will send someone to feed us and give us exactly what we need to make it through life's journey.

God has already prepared a strengthening for us, and it will get us through our current situation, just like it did Elijah.

Come Out of the Cave

Depression makes us want to run and hide from life's problems. Our fears, hurts, and pains cause us to withdraw into ourselves and be alone. But social isolation can be a terrible thing. Anything left alone will eventually deteriorate. Consider what happens to an abandoned car, house, or yard. In the same manner, we begin to show signs of neglect just like they do.

When I struggled with depression, my emotions got the best of me. I went into an emotional cave by hiding and isolating myself from others. Though I intended for it to be a resting place from the world's cares, it became so comfortable the cave ended up being my hiding place. I just wanted to stay there and not see anyone. I missed church, family events, and all the other social gatherings I had previously enjoyed. While hiding made me feel better initially and gave me a sense of winning, I later realized it was only a false sense of security, and I ended up feeling defeated even more.

Even when depressed, God does not call us to hide. He calls us to go.

"And he said unto them, Go ye into all the world, and preach the gospel to every creature" (Mark 16:15).

Hiding keeps us from confronting our problems. We will only be protected and in a safe place when in the will of God. Hiding in a cave does not align with God's plans for our lives.

"And he came thither unto a cave, and lodged there; and, behold, the word of the LORD came to him, and he said unto him, What doest thou here, Elijah?" (1 Kings 19:9).

When God asked Elijah why he was in the cave, He already knew Elijah's answer. But He wanted Elijah to realize he was hiding out and to question his why. God asks us the same question today. What are you doing here? Why did you isolate yourself and forget about me? Elijah came to himself, left the cave, and got back to serving the Lord.

When we feel down, we have to pick ourselves up. God still sits high up on the throne and is able to comfort us. Today God calls us out of our caves and depressive mind-sets. He says, don't go low, but come up higher. For we have overextended our stays, and our cave seasons are over.

God Wants to Speak

Loss of perspective lies at the heart of depression. When we face seemingly impossible problems and feel hemmed in, we doubt God can make a way and become depressed.

When I struggled with depression, I had this one-sided view of things. *I give up. I will never be happy. This relationship is not working, and it will never work.* I made myself miserable with all the negative talk. I finally stopped talking and started listening to God. When I looked around, I had a fresh perspective on life. I had to allow God to speak to me.

After Elijah got his rest and nourishment, God took him up on a mountain and spoke to him.

> *And he said, I have been very zealous for the LORD God of hosts: because the children of Israel have forsaken thy covenant, thrown down thine altars, and slain thy prophets with the sword; and I, even I only, am left; and they seek my life, to take it away. And the LORD said unto him, Go, return on thy way to the wilderness of Damascus: and when thou comest, anoint Hazael to be king over Syria: And Jehu the son of Nimshi shalt thou anoint to be king over Israel: and Elisha the son of Shaphat of Abel-meholah shalt thou anoint to be prophet in thy room. And it shall come to pass, that him that escapeth the sword of Hazael shall Jehu slay: and him that escapeth from the sword of Jehu shall Elisha slay. Yet I have left me seven thousand in Israel, all the knees which have not bowed unto Baal, and every mouth which hath not kissed him. (1 Kings 19:14–18).*

Depression makes us think we are all alone, and Elijah felt the same way. God comforted Elijah by speaking to him with His still small voice. Refreshed after spending time with God, Elijah gained a new perspective. After God comforted Elijah, He ministered to him. Elijah thought he was the only one left but found out there were seven thousand prophets preserved in Israel.

After God talked to Elijah and gave him a new outlook, he was ready to go on to anoint kings. When distracted by the pain of depression, God wants to speak to us, no matter how far down we spiral. Remember, He waits to speak to us and give us a new look, new vision, and new level.

The Lifter of My Head

There are so many things which can cause us to fell discouraged and defeated. During those times, we become sad and hang our heads. But God does not want us to live depressed and discouraged. He wants us to enjoy life. Our outlooks can change when we look to God and let Him lift us up.

I have noticed while attending to daily business, sometimes I walk with my head down, which feels uncomfortable. When I catch myself hanging my head, I am usually in deep thought, worrying, or discouraged about something. I can actually feel the weight of the world on my shoulders. Plus, I realize it's not wise to look down because I could run into someone or something. I am grateful His Word reminds us of God's power.

> "But thou, O LORD, art a shield for me; my glory,
> and the lifter up of mine head" (Ps. 3:3).

This word ministered to me when I needed it most. When problems arise, and the cares of this world drag me down, I remember God is with me. We can stand tall, throw our shoulders back, and hold our heads up in confidence knowing God never leaves us. God loves us so much. Even today, in the mist of our trials, He still stands as the lifter of our heads.

Why Sit Here and Die?

Depression can bring all kinds of disturbing thoughts of death. We all probably know or have heard of someone taking their lives after battling depression. Painful emotions overwhelm people who feel suicidal, and they see death as their only escape. They lose sight of the fact suicide provides a permanent solution to a temporary condition. Sadly, most people who die by suicide could have been helped. No matter how bad the problems we face appear or how deeply buried under life's circumstances we seem to be, we can get back on top.

At one time I worried about dying and became so hopeless I feared I would become suicidal. Later, I realized my obsessions centered on my problems and not God. I had pushed God out of sight because I allowed myself to be influenced by the wrong voice. My faith had subsided, and life caved in from every side. It took a lot of strength, but I managed to push through those dark thoughts. I stopped crying and forced myself to move forward. Again, I looked myself in the mirror and said, "If you don't get up and do something, you are not going to make it. Why should you live cooped up when God has given you freedom? You can't just sit here and die!"

The Bible gives us a great illustration of how to overcome a dying situation. The story of the four lepers gives us an invaluable lesson of how to overcome depression.

> *And there were four leprous men at the entering in of the gate: and they said one to another, why sit we here until we die? If we say, we will enter into the city, then the famine is in the city, and we shall die there: and if we sit still here, we die also. Now therefore come and let us fall unto the host of the Syrians: if they save us alive, we shall live; and if they kill us, we shall but die. And they rose up in the twilight, to go unto the camp of the Syrians: and when they were come to the uttermost part of the camp of Syria, behold, there was no man there. (2 Kings 7:3–5).*

The four lepers sat, dying of starvation. They could have given up on life, but they didn't. Instead of waiting to die, they decided to take their chances and go into the enemy's camp. When they got there, they found it abandoned. All the warriors had been frightened away by the angels of God, and they'd left enough food behind to feed all of Samaria. God turned the entire situation around.

God also promises to turn your dark clouds into sunny days. So don't just sit there until you die! Don't accept defeat. Cast off those feelings of doom and gloom. You can get back up and receive deliverance from the Lord.

Unwrapping the Grave Clothes

I believe many people stay wrapped in the clothes of death. Depression can cause us to fall into a deep slumber and prevent us from living the life we were called to do. It's a spiritual death where some slumber, not realizing they are dead. The time has come for us to remove our death clothes and put on clothes which bring us life.

When I think back over my life and how God delivered me from depressive thoughts, my heart floods with joy. I could have died. Sometimes, I felt like dying, but I thank God I didn't. God came in just the nick of time to rescue me from the hands of death and destruction. I had to come out of the tomb of sorrow and regret. I took off the graves clothes and mourning garments of what had happened and embraced what God was doing. A new life stood in front of me as I shook off the dust and looked to the future.

Unwrapping my grave clothes reminded me of the biblical story of Lazarus and how the Lord Himself had called him to come out of death and into life.

> *"And when he thus had spoken, he cried with a loud voice, Lazarus, come forth. And he that was dead came forth, bound hand and foot with grave clothes: and his face was bound about with a napkin. Jesus saith unto them, loose him, and let him go" (John 11:43–44).*

When God called Lazarus forth, he abandoned the grave clothes which wrapped his body and received the new clothes of life. God took death away from him, and Lazarus went forth.

Right now, God is breathing life back into those situations we thought were dead. He can revive our situations which look dark, dim, and beyond repair. He has resurrection power and can bring life back to our health, marriages, finances, etc. God calls us to come into the light and to come forth as Lazarus did. As we lose the grave clothes, He will give us the clothing of new life.

Put on Some Praise

Praise is one of the greatest spiritual keys to help overcome depression, for praise gets our focus on God, not our problems. Depressed people focus on the negative so much until those things become bigger in their lives.

I keep a magnifying glass in my office to remind me of the nature of praise as it relates to depression. When depressed, we zoom in on the bad things, which keep us down in the pit. Like a magnifying glass, praise causes what we focus on to get bigger, to be magnified. When praising God, we magnify the problem solver, not our problems.

During my days of depression, I had a wrong impression about praise. I thought I was supposed to wait until I had no problems and felt better before I gave God the praise. I didn't know praise led to eliminating those horrible feelings. When I began to praise God with my heavy heart, I experienced a new sense of hope and joy. Through praising God, I was reminded God is bigger than any situation I face. Now when I sense negative feelings coming on, I cut them off by putting on praise, as if I were wearing a nice warm sweater in the winter time. Actually, Isaiah talks about putting on the garment of praise when we feel heavy.

> "To appoint unto them that mourn in Zion, to give unto them beauty for ashes, the oil of joy for mourning, the garment of praise for the spirit of heaviness; that they might be called trees of righteousness, the planting of the LORD, that he might be glorified" (Isa. 61:3).

A garment of praise is a piece of clothing we put on to cover our spirits. When we feel downcast, cloudy, and depressed, a spirit of heaviness can become dislodged in our attitudes and in our hearts. Wrapping ourselves in the garment of praise covers our spirits and takes away the heaviness. But a garment of praise differs from other garments we own. We wear it on the inside of us, not the outside. And the praise garment is the only one designed by God. It's the right size to cover and replace the spirit of heaviness. So next time you feel down, put on some praise.

There Is Hope

One of the common threads of depressed people is they lose hope. They think nothing will change or things will only get worse. But what defines hope? Hope is not, "I hope it doesn't rain because I want to go to the football game." Nor does hope simply wish for the best to happen. Our hope lies in knowing.

When I lived in a state of despair, I felt like nothing would improve. I had no confidence because I listened to the enemy's lies, which said I didn't have a chance, that I would always feel this way. In order to overcome, I had to pull down this stronghold of unbelief and refuse to sorrow as one who had no hope. I rejected all pessimism and refused to have a heart of a skeptic. I believed I stood only steps away from my breakthrough. For I had confidence in knowing something good would happen for me.

> *"And now, Lord, what wait I for? My hope is in thee" (Ps. 39:7).*

When King David was down and discouraged, he remembered his savior in the midst of his sorrows. He knew who to turn to for hope, the God of our lives and the rock of our salvation.

Like King David, we can have confidence in knowing something good is coming our way, because our hope remains rooted and grounded in the Lord. We can't find this kind of hope in people or things, for the world can't give us the peace we need when faced with great difficulties. Thankfully, we don't have to simply fade away when we feel blue. We have hope because God gives us promises, they are yes and amen. It's not, "We hope it happens for us," rather, "We know it will come to pass." Instead of lying down in a hopeless situation, we can stand on the promises of God.

13

According to Your Faith

The world doesn't really understand faith. I compare the confusion to having a high-tech smart phone and knowing its potential, but not having a clue about how to use it. We think faith is a feeling, but faith satisfies us so much more. While we all may have faith, all of us may not believe, trust, and rely on God by taking action. Faith will require us to act on what we believe in order to receive the blessings of God. In other words, we will receive according to our faith.

"Now faith is the substance of things hoped for, the evidence of things not seen" (Heb. 11:1).

Faith is not based upon what we see. Faith overrides the natural and changes what we see into what we want. Faith calls forth from the invisible realm into the physical realm. Like a magnet, it pulls the promises of God into our earthly situations. Faith doesn't see what we see. While we see wounded, faith sees mended. While we see broken, faith sees wholeness. While we see defeat, faith sees victory.

Years ago, if I had done something according to my faith, nothing would have happened. When challenges came, I muddled through life trying to determine the outcome. I struggled and therefore did not receive from heaven because I lacked faith. I tried to figure things out in my head. But faith doesn't live in the head—it resides in the heart. I had to trust God and His Word to overcome the obstacles in my way. I couldn't receive my blessings based on my spouse's faith or my pastor's faith. I had to receive according to my faith. I had to receive according to what the Lord said to me and what I needed in my life.

The Bible has many instances of people receiving according to their faith. The story of two blind men is one of those examples.

> *And when Jesus departed thence, two blind men followed him, crying, and saying, Thou son of David, have mercy on us. And when he was come into the house, the blind men came to him: and Jesus saith unto them, believe ye that I am able to do this? They said unto him, Yea, LORD. Then touched he their eyes, saying, according to your faith be it unto you. And their eyes were opened; and Jesus straitly charged them, saying, see that no man know it. (Matt. 9:27–30).*

When the two blind men went to Jesus, He asked if they believed He could heal them. They said yes, then Jesus touched their eyes, and they were healed. They received their healing according to their faith. In other words, Jesus responded to their faith and opened their eyes. We can all live the abundant life promised to us and enjoy all the blessings of God, but we will not be able to get them with our talents or good looks. We will only be able to obtain them according to our faith.

Believing God

People all over the world clothe themselves in special garments, deny themselves the necessities of life, and spend much time in prayer in an effort to make themselves acceptable and pleasing to God. This may be okay, but the greatest thing we can do to please God is to believe Him.

My faith was a key component in God's process of healing my hurts. Although my healing did not come instantly, it did come. I believed for my healing, and I accepted it by faith. I had never been to Alaska, and yet I believed it exists. How did I know? I know because someone told me, and I also read about it. I accepted it by faith. Without questioning it, I chose to believe. So it is with God. I believed Him and accepted Him by faith.

Our world's belief system may frown upon someone who says they believe God and surrenders what they have in order to get something better. But this is exactly what Abraham did.

> *"And he believed in the LORD; and he counted it to him for righteousness" (Gen. 15:6).*

Abraham believed God to the greatest degree. He obeyed, left his home, and traveled to a foreign land. He did something many of us could not do: pack up and leave everything behind. And if that weren't enough, he was willing to give up his son, Isaac, when God asked him to. We have to believe God, even when most of the world thinks we are crazy. We have to believe and stand in faith against all odds.

Perhaps you stand against a broken marriage, a terminal illness, or another trying situation. Keep believing and trusting in God. Even when He asks for your Isaacs, be willing to obey God, believing He will provide. He will move every obstacle out of your way and send His miracle power to work on your behalf. This you can believe.

When Faith Is Shaken

When the trials of life break our hearts and steal our peace, we often find ourselves in panic mode. We know what God has done for us in the past, but in times of desperation, we forget what we know. We find ourselves in a state of shock when the trials of life show us no mercy.

I have tasted God's goodness and have enjoyed close fellowship with Him. I have felt His power and His love. Yet, in the midst of profound pain and struggle, sometimes I have felt alone and afraid. My faith had been shaken. When I hurt, I felt as though God had left me and I stood on shaky ground. Yet God had a method to all the mess. Although I couldn't see the plan at the time, God knew what He was doing even when I didn't. There was a purpose in the shaking. The shaking of my faith made me more aware of the condition of my faith. When the shaking came, everything which could be shaken fell. The shaking exposed a foundation in my life which needed strengthening and repair.

So what do we do when life tumbles around us and the ground beneath us nearly collapses? It's during these times of uncertainty we need to hold on to God and stand firm on the foundation of His promises. Once the shaking ends, everything which remains will be secured. When our faith is shaken and the ground beneath us shifts, we can stand on the Word of God when things seem out of reach.

> *Whosoever cometh to me, and heareth my sayings, and doeth them, I will shew you to whom he is like: He is like a man which built an house, and digged deep, and laid the foundation on a rock: and when the flood arose, the stream beat vehemently upon that house, and could not shake it: for it was founded upon a rock. (Luke 6:47–48).*

When the storms of life threaten our faith and we don't know where to go, we can go to the rock, Jesus Christ. For when we stand on the rock, although the winds may beat against us and the waves may be breaking on the shore of our lives, we will not be moved. We will not be shaken because we are standing on the rock, which is stronger than we will ever envision.

Overcoming Failures by Faith

Facing failures can be difficult. It's not always easy to admit we have messed up. Sometimes we just give up in the face of failures. Have you ever thought about doing this? Maybe you failed at work and now you want to quit and go look for another job. Or perhaps you failed in school and instead of working harder or getting a tutor, you dropped out.

Oftentimes, we look at our failures as death, or the final wrap up. So we might as well surrender and call it quits.

I have had a lot of success in life, but I have also had some failures. Some of those failures were small, and others rather significant, as failing in marriage. Those failures could have defined my life and demolished me completely, but they didn't. I continued in faith and found my full potential God predestined for me. Overcoming my failures wasn't always easy, but I used my faith and believed God would still help me in spite of my mishaps. I could have checked out and gone home.

When I think of using faith to overcome failures, I look at Moses.

> *And it came to pass in those days, when Moses was grown, that he went out unto his brethren, and looked on their burdens: and he spied an Egyptian smiting an Hebrew, one of his brethren. And he looked this way and that way, and when he saw that there was no man, he slew the Egyptian, and hid him in the sand. And when he went out the second day, behold, two men of the Hebrews strove together: and he said to him that did the wrong, wherefore smitest thou thy fellow? And he said, who made thee a prince and judge over us? Intendest thou to kill me, as thou killedst the Egyptian? And Moses feared, and said, surely this thing is known. (Exod. 2:11–14).*

Moses had done a terrible thing when he killed a Hebrew slave. But Moses didn't go home because he had messed up. He could have allowed the crime to define the rest of his life, but he didn't. Moses could have given up and walked away from the whole thing, but he endured. Years later, he stepped out in faith and went back to lead the Israelites out of Egypt.

When life pushes us into a corner and our backs against the wall, we can come through with ease if we use our faith. Faith ignites the power to overcome failures.

Speak to Your Mountain

Anything which blocks us slows us down or stops us from progressing in life is a mountain. Many times, instead of using our faith, we spend a lot of time complaining about our mountains, crying, and moaning about how they hinder us. We talk about our mountains, but in order to have complete victory, we have to stop talking about them and start talking to them.

I haven't always effectively handled the mountains in my life . . . pain and adversity, debt, disappointments, etc. I didn't know I had to speak to them to move them out of my way. I would pray and ask God to speak to them for me or send someone else to speak to them. But I had to use my faith and start speaking to the problems in my life. And as I spoke and believed what I said, my mountains dwindled to nothing. They only served as a stepping stone into God's great plan for my life. Since I thought only God has the authority, I asked Him to take care of my mountains, but He showed me I also had authority to take out my own mountains.

The Bible tells us about it in the book of Mark.

> "For verily I say unto you, That whosoever shall say unto this mountain, Be thou removed, and be thou cast into the sea; and shall not doubt in his heart, but shall believe that those things which he saith shall come to pass; he shall have whatsoever he saith" (Mark 11:23).

According to Mark, God has given all of us the authority to move mountains. People with authority, use it by speaking. We have been given the authority over everything as we speak in faith. We have the power to operate in the God kind of faith. He desires for us to be delivered from this present world of troubles. He does not want us to live subject to the world's standards. We no longer have to be held back or held up. As you act on God's Word and start speaking to your situations, you will have mountain-moving faith. Stand up against the mountains in your life and say, "Be removed."

Faith in the Fire

We all face situations in our daily lives which challenge our faith and submission to God. Often when placed in a threatening, heated environment, our faith is put to the test of whether we will obey God first and foremost or yield to the pressure to conform to some other standard. When we wake up and find ourselves in the middle of a hot pursuit with scorching temperatures, we need faith to help us face the fire.

I tried to keep the faith when things got heated up in my life. I trusted God and stood on His Word. But instead of things getting better, they got worse. The pressure increased. I had to make a choice. I could surrender and cave in or stay in the place of faith and trust God. He gave me the strength to stand against the pressures of life and fight in faith. I stayed in the fire, believing God would deliver me and bring me through every heated battle.

The story of Shadrach, Meshach, and Abednego demonstrates great faith. Fully committed to God, these men didn't allow anything to make them bow to Nebuchadnezzar's god. Even in the fire, they still had faith in God.

> *And these three men, Shadrach, Meshach, and Abednego, fell down bound into the midst of the burning fiery furnace. Then Nebuchadnezzar the king was astonished, and rose up in haste, and spake, and said unto his counsellors, did not we cast three men bound into the midst of the fire? They answered and said unto the king, True, O king. He answered and said, Lo, I see four men loose, walking in the midst of the fire, and they have no hurt; and the form of the fourth*

134

is like the Son of God. Then Nebuchadnezzar came near to the mouth of the burning fiery furnace, and spake, and said, Shadrach, Meshach, and Abednego, ye servants of the most high God, come forth, and come hither. Then Shadrach, Meshach, and Abednego, came forth of the midst of the fire. And the princes, governors, and captains, and the king's counsellors, being gathered together, saw these men, upon whose bodies the fire had no power, nor was an hair of their head singed, neither were their coats changed, nor the smell of fire had passed on them. (Dan. 3:23–27).

How different our lives would be if everyone had the kind of faith in God as these three men! When the fires of life threatened them, they didn't lose heart. God delivered Shadrach, Meshach, and Abednego, and He will do the same for you. Have faith to stand firm and know, even if you are thrown into the fiery furnace, God will be the fourth man in your fire. You will come out without even the smell of smoke.

When Faith Touches God

Many people say they follow God, but only a few have touched Him with their faith. Oftentimes when we hurt, we do not have enough faith in God to go after Him with every fiber of our being. We play it safe, because we don't want to make a scene and draw attention to ourselves. We want everyone to think we have it all together. When desperate, we have to use our faith and reach out to God. For just one simple touch from God will be powerful enough to heal, restore, and set us free.

I had been suffering with things for many years and desperately needed a touch from God. My heart bled from a fatal blow in relationships and other tragic situations in my life. But I needed more than just an ordinary touch. I needed a touch which would change my life, a touch of healing and deliverance. I believed if I touched God with my faith, His power would be released on my behalf.

When thinking about God's healing touch, I couldn't help but think about the woman in the Bible who had the issue of blood.

> *And a certain woman, which had an issue of blood twelve years, And had suffered many things of many physicians, and had spent all that she had, and was nothing bettered, but rather grew worse, When she had heard of Jesus, came in the press behind, and touched his garment. For she said, if I may touch but his clothes, I shall be whole. And straightway the fountain of her blood was dried up; and she felt in her body that she was healed of that plague. And Jesus, immediately knowing in himself that virtue had gone out of him, turned him about in the press, and said, who touched my clothes? And his disciples said unto him, thou seest the multitude thronging thee, and sayest thou, who touched me? And he looked round about to see her that had done this thing. But the woman fearing and trembling, knowing what was done in her, came and fell down before him, and told him all the truth. And he said unto her, Daughter, thy faith hath made thee whole; go in peace and be whole of thy plague. (Mark 5:25–34).*

After reading the above Scripture, I realized I, too, could reach beyond what I saw. When I faced the next crisis and all of hell had come against me, I exercised faith and refused to back down. I withstood the opposition and allowed my faith to touch God. I kept pressing in and through. And as my faith touched Him, He noticed me and came to my rescue.

Whatever your situation, you, too, can be healed just like me and the woman with the issue of blood. She pushed through her pain and reached out to touch God, even if she only touched just a piece of His clothing. Although her situation seemed hopeless, she pressed through the crowd. And when she touched Him, not only was she healed, but made whole.

Move Forward in Faith

When faced with tough situations and treading in foreign territory, we tend to want to turn and go back to familiar ground. Although we left a dreadful and painful past, fear of the unknown frightens us. With any new situation comes potential for discomfort and a sense of loss. We start thinking about all the things which could go wrong in our new lives and then we start back peddling.

Change can be scary. I know it was for me. Yes, I was sick and tired of my previous situation and had actually escaped from under its weight. But then I started having thoughts of what-ifs which kept me from walking into a better reality. I remember trying to convince myself things weren't so bad after all and I could deal with the situation a little longer. But deep down, I knew if I was going to enjoy a flourishing life, I would have to leave my comfort zone and get over into the faith zone. I had to move forward in faith.

The children of Israel had a similar ordeal when leaving their place of bondage.

> *"And the LORD said unto Moses, wherefore criest thou unto me? Speak unto the children of Israel, that they go forward" (Exod. 14:15).*

The children of Israel had been delivered from Egypt, but they wanted to go back. Instead of using their faith to move on, they were influenced by fear. They panicked and wanted to go back to the very thing which had held them bound for more than four hundred years! But God specifically tells us He is displeased when we turn back.

> *"Now the just shall live by faith: but if any man draws back, my soul shall have no pleasure in him" (Heb. 10:38).*

Like the Israelites, we can't go back to Egypt or some other place in our past. I know we may have some uncertainty about where we are or where we are going, but we have to move forward in faith. God will not be pleased with us if we turn back.

God moves in our lives by faith. When the children of Israel stepped into the water, the Red Sea stood in their path blocking them from their promised land. With Pharaoh's army in hot pursuit, God parted the sea, so the Israelites could arrive safely on the other side. Then, at just the right time, He closed the entry point and destroyed Pharaoh's army. When we trust God and put our feet on faith, whatever held us back will separate and divide. Keep walking forward in faith, and God will make a way for a miracle.

Faith Works with Patience

We receive from God by faith, but our faith has to be undergirded by patience. It takes faith and patience to survive in this world. God's timing usually differs from ours. When God tells us something, we have to exercise faith and be patient to see it through. If we become impatient, we can delay God's best for us, which can cost us dearly.

This is exactly what happened with Abraham and Sarah. God promised them a son, but after years of waiting, Abraham grew weary and ended up doing as Sarah suggested and had a child by Hagar, her servant.

I, too, have also become anxious and made some costly mistakes. Just like Sarah, I devised some kind of plan to help God, because it seemed He was running late or had forgotten all about me. My mistakes happened because I didn't understand God's timetable. When I ask God for something and He tells me I can have it, I want it to arrive right away. When going through my season of suffering, things didn't work out according to my plan. I prayed, spoke words of faith, and did whatever else I could to try to hold on. But as time went by, it seemed the words of faith no longer worked, and I thought I needed to do something about it.

> *"That ye be not slothful, but followers of them who through faith and patience inherit the promises"* *(Heb. 6:12).*

Faith, mixed with patience, will help us to receive God's blessings. We need both because God's timing is everything. Just because the blessing hasn't arrived, doesn't mean it's not coming. If Sarah had known this, she would have saved herself some trouble. For when we try to help God out, negative consequences emerge.

In Sarah's case, she became jealous and hated Hagar for doing what she had wanted her to do. The mistake of having Ishmael and not waiting for Isaac still affects our nations today. As illustrated by what happened to Abraham and Sarah when they intervened, we need to have patience and wait on God. He knows what's best for us. For when we are patient, we receive His promises for our lives.

Can You Use a Faith Lift?

Is your faith in need of repair? Have the stress and problems of life taken a toll on your faith? Just like aging skin, our faith can lose its strength. It can become worn out, full of worry wrinkles, and look dull. But there is hope for a sagging faith.

My faith was once so weak and dry, but once I started supplying it with a steady diet of God's Word, I became infused with hydration from heaven. No longer dry and lifeless, my faith rose to a higher dimension in God. For when I meditated on the Word, I noticed my faith began to grow. My faith in God's Word has enabled me to thrive in an unfavorable environment.

> *"So then faith cometh by hearing, and hearing by the word of God"* *(Rom. 10:17).*

The Word of God demonstrates acts of faith, which lift us up. I used to close my Bible and pray for faith. Now I open it, study the

Word, and my faith lifts to a deeper dimension. Our faith will be renewed and refreshed when we meditate on the Word of God. This is vital to season and strengthen our faith, so we can stand against life's problems and struggles.

14

Discovering the Holy Spirit

I grew up in a Christian church-going family. We talked a lot about Jesus and who He is but had only limited conversations devoted to the Holy Spirit. When I first heard the story about Pentecost, my reaction for a long time was, "That must have been an electrifying experience for those in the upper room, with all those flames hovering above their heads and people speaking in a heavenly language." I knew the Holy Spirit was real, but I never thought much more about it until I met the Holy Spirit as a real person and He did something similar in me.

In 2005, I felt so empty and hollow in side. I loved the Lord but spiritually, sensed life offered more. I hungered for something to fill me with zeal and enthusiasm. In my quest to find the "something," I attended a revival at a neighborhood church. The speaker talked about encountering the Holy Spirit in a new and deeper way. Initially, I felt uncomfortable with this type of message. I hadn't heard anything like it before, plus I thought I received all of the Holy Spirit when I accepted Jesus at a young age. I didn't realize a deeper relationship with the Holy Spirit existed.

As the preacher delved deeper into the message, I found myself opening up a little more despite my discomfort. As I bent my ear to the sermon, I came to understand more about the baptism of the Holy Spirit. Up to this point, I had only witnessed a small portion of His work. I understood this experience to be more like a big "dunk" in the Holy Spirit, which gives power to overcome life's obstacles, peace in the midst of tough times, and a helper during prayer time. I began thinking, "I am not sure what it is, but I need it in my life."

At the sermon's conclusion, the preacher gave an altar call for those who desired to receive the baptism of the Holy Spirit. I felt I had heard enough about the Holy Spirit and now wanted to receive this powerful gift. I thought I was ready, but I couldn't gather up enough faith to march to the altar. Fear had me glued to the pew. So I just sat there and gazed from a distance. What I saw happen next left me speechless. As the preacher started to minister to people, they began to speak in a different language and worship God. I began to feel uneasy, as if I had missed my opportunity to receive this awesome gift. But the preacher assured me I could still have it. He encouraged me to go home and study the book of Acts and ask God to fill me with his precious Holy Spirit. He said if I did this, I would be filled. I believed Him.

I went home, read Acts, and asked God to fill me just as the preacher recommended. A few days later, while listening to another gospel preacher's sermon about the Holy Spirit, I began to feel a stirring inside of me. Shortly after, I felt something slowly moving in my abdominal region. I didn't recognize the feeling, but this movement became more noticeable and started moving inside of me, approaching my chest. Sensing something about to happen, I got up and closed the door.

After returning to my seat, I heard a noise which sounded like a strong wind. Before I could gather myself, this presence made a grand entrance into the room. While I don't remember all the experience's details, I do remember falling on the floor. And when I came to myself, I spoke in a heavenly language. I had experienced my very own Pentecost.

A Special Kind of Friend

What kind of friends do you have? Are your friends honest? Do they tell you the truth even when it hurts? Do your friends love you and care about you and your problems? We all have friends who have been there for us. They have helped us get through tough times just by being there. I have friends who have been there for me. The Holy Spirit is that kind of friend.

I have never met anyone quite like Him. He understands me and cares about my problems. He knows just what I need. I am a better person because of Him, for He has filled my life with love. He has helped me tremendously through His comfort and friendship. He's a gentle guy and a very sensitive person. For He is saddened when I say or do things I shouldn't. But although sometimes I make Him sad, He isn't weak. He's full of power and cares so much about me. With the Holy Spirit as my friend, I don't have to be lonely or helpless again.

> *"And I will pray the Father, and he shall give you another Comforter, that he may abide with you forever" (John 14:16).*

Jesus loves me so much that He sent His Holy Spirit to be my special friend. Jesus became a friend to all who wanted His friendship, but a human body limited Jesus. He could only be in one place at a time. He couldn't get to all of His friends who needed Him. This explains why the Holy Spirit is so special to us. He is another comforter, one who consoles us when we hurt and can be with us all at the same time, wherever we go.

Power to Witness

A computer has the potential to do all it was created to do, but it has no real power on its own. It must be "powered" up in order to be effective. When we are filled with the Holy Spirit, we tap into a power source. When it comes down to defeating our giants and overcoming obstacles in life, we will be more effective if we have the power of the Holy Spirit.

When I became filled with the Holy Spirit, one of the first things I noticed was an inner strength and ability. This inner strength gave me the power to keep going when I wanted to give up. It felt as if someone on the inside cheered me on. I also noticed an ability to minister to others began to flow. The Holy Spirit guided me and told me what to say to help. I found out witnessing to others was one of the main reasons for having the Holy Spirit. This was Jesus's divine plan for worldwide evangelism. The Lord knew the Holy Spirit would give me power to do whatever necessary to carry out His will.

> *"But you will receive power when the Holy Spirit comes upon you. And you will be my witnesses, telling people about me everywhere—in Jerusalem, throughout Judea, in Samaria, and to the ends of the earth" (Acts 1:8, NLT).*

People who have been healed, delivered, and set free from tragic lives can be very effective witnesses with the Holy Spirit. The Holy Spirit has given me courage to share my insights, struggles, and how I am doing today. I have been able to uplift and encourage others by the strength of the Holy Spirit. I don't rely on my own strength, rather I lean on the transforming power of the Holy Spirit to bring about internal changes in the hearts and lives of people. It takes courage to share my faith and to witness to the lost. Satan has tried to do everything he could to hinder me. He has power, but it is no match for the power of the Holy Spirit.

Showing Me Things to Come

Have you ever been surprised by some life event and thought, "I never saw it coming"? Have you wondered why someone didn't warn you before things got out of hand? How wonderful would it be to know what's around the corner and what's coming up the road!

Having the Holy Spirit helps us to know these things. The Holy Spirit knows what happened in our past, and He can also show us what is coming up ahead. For the Holy Spirit knows everything, including exactly what will happen to us.

Last year I had a vision of a black funeral car coming up my parents' driveway and sure enough, it happened just like I saw it. God warned me because He knows the future and wanted to prepare me. He gave me a vision, so I would not be caught off guard. Sometimes He speaks to me in dreams, and sometimes it's through His Word as He impresses Scriptures upon my heart. There have been times when I just decided for some reason to go a different way and later found out there was an accident on my usual route. God is always showing me something. I just have to be aware and open to Him.

> *"Howbeit when he, the Spirit of truth, is come, he will guide you into all truth: for he shall not speak of himself; but whatsoever he shall hear, that shall he speak: and he will shew you things to come" (John 16:13).*

When someone tells you, they have all the answers and know exactly what you need to do, you can tell them Jesus said differently. Jesus said the Holy Spirit will show us things to come. He knows everything and does not try to hide anything from us. He has placed His Holy Spirit in us, so we can know what lies before us.

A Move of the Holy Spirit

We are all in desperate need of God moving in our lives. When we think of moving, actions like changing church membership, moving to another house or relocating to another town may come to mind. But God moves in a much more powerful way, on the inside. The Holy Spirit is like a special medical team for those who have especially deep wounds. For He desires to bring inner healing and completeness to those who have been hurt. He wants to move in our lives to bring about change and to develop a deeper relationship with us.

When the Holy Spirit came into my life, He started moving in me, which brought about change. He moved upon my heart to repent when I did wrong, to forgive those who wronged me, to love more, and to go after God with more zeal. The Holy Spirit moves hearts. Without the Holy Spirit working in my life, everything remained at a standstill, as if I were held back by a dam. But when the Holy Spirit came in, everything began to flow. The bursting of the dams caused a move of the Spirit for everyone to see.

> *"And the earth was without form, and void; and darkness was upon the face of the deep. And the Spirit of God moved upon the face of the waters"* (Gen. 1:2).

The Word of God opens with the moving of the Holy Spirit. The Holy Spirit was the first mover and continues to move on our behalf. He is able to overcome any boundaries and move walls of hearts. He wants to move us from lack to abundance, from the back to the front. He does not come so we can remain stagnant, rather he comes to work and move mightily in our lives.

A Prayer Partner

Whom do you go to for help when you feel trapped, cornered, or pinned against the wall? In moments like these, do you feel overwhelmed with a sense of desperation, or do you know where to turn? The Holy Spirit is available to help us every day in times when we feel backed into a corner by life's situations.

One of the areas where the Holy Spirit has been most helpful to me is in my prayer life. Prior to my encounter with the Holy Spirit, I didn't have much of a prayer life. I thought I could handle life without God, but I can't. My natural wisdom doesn't always get the job done in those tough situations. Besides, when distracted by pain, I find it difficult to concentrate on prayer. I love partnering with the Holy Spirit in prayer, for He comes along beside me and helps me. He comforts me, speaks to me, and strengthens me. He helps bare my burdens. It's like He says, "Climb on my back, and

I will carry you. We will walk and pray together." I pray by Him, through Him, and in Him.

> "And the Holy Spirit helps us in our weakness. For example, we don't know what God wants us to pray for. But the Holy Spirit prays for us with groanings that cannot be expressed in words" (Rom. 8:26, NLT).

We need the Holy Spirit to pray for us according to our needs, our dangers, and His desires for us. We don't know what's best for us when we are in dire situations. When I didn't have a clue what to pray, He did. He has given me wisdom and strength when I needed it most. My prayers have become more satisfying and meaningful. I can't fail in life when I depend on the best prayer partner in the world.

The Spirit of Counsel

People constantly look for answers about their lives but often seek it through misguided means such as horoscopes and other unscriptural sources. Instead of confiding in worldly resources for answers to our problems, we can receive spiritual therapy by the Holy Spirit. For only the Holy Spirit knows God's will for our lives, and He serves as our counselor to guide us toward our destinies. Think of the Holy Spirit as our personal guidance counselor, He directs us and help us to make godly choices.

> "And the spirit of the LORD shall rest upon him, the spirit of wisdom and understanding, the spirit of counsel and might, the spirit of knowledge and of the fear of the LORD" (Isa. 11:2).

The Spirit of Counsel has been like a personal advisor in my life. He tells me what I should and shouldn't do. I don't need to move an inch without the friendly counsel of the Lord. When life gets complicated and twisted, I go to the Holy Spirit for help and support. His directions and guidance has prevented me from making mistakes and has empowered me to overcome past mistakes.

"Where no counsel is, the people fall: but in the multitude of counsellors there is safety" (Prov. 11:14).

People stumble and fall when there is no counsel. I don't want to fall. I want to be sure of my steps, not wandering around in circles. With counsel from the Holy Spirit, I am able to see God's way clearly and know His thoughts toward me. Life can be a maze, but the Spirit of Counsel will come and help us navigate the maze of life.

Living under the Influence

All of us like to be happy, to feel good, and to be on top of things. There's nothing wrong with that. God wants us all to be joyful, happy, and uplifted people. The problem lies in what generates happiness. Some people think they will find happiness in a liquid bottle or in a narcotic, but neither of those will bring lasting joy.

There is a strong connection with being intoxicated with wine and being intoxicated with the Holy Spirit. The similarity is they are both powerful and controlling agents. When we drink excessively, the alcohol controls our behaviors which take us into potentially dangerous territory. When we are influenced by the Holy Spirit, we continually surrender our minds, bodies, and time to His control. Every area of our lives is affected when the Spirit fills us.

I remember looking at the old Western movies. If a snake bit a cowboy, he took a drink of alcohol to numb the pain. Being filled with the Spirit has a similar effect. When I am controlled by the Spirit and people talk about me, mistreat me, or wrong me, I will not feel the pain. People may say false things about me, but if I am living under the influence, I can love my enemies and pray for them. When I am living under the influence, although still in pain, I can praise

God. The indwelling of the Holy Spirit enables me to laugh with joy even in depressing situations.

People usually get loud when under the influence of alcohol, and they can be difficult to quiet down. When I am living under the influence of the Spirit, I make a joyful noise. I tell folks about God's goodness, what He has done for me, how He turned my life around, and how He protected me even when I didn't know my life stood in harm's way. Sometimes I just start shouting and praising God, because I live under the influence. The Spirit-filled life overflows with joy, gratitude, and good behavior, quite the opposite of a life enslaved to alcohol.

An increasing number of people believe drinking alcohol provides happiness. People drink to feel better and for a "happy" hour. But I need to be filled with something which will last longer than an hour. Some people drink so much until they become highly intoxicated, but Paul tells us there is a better way to cope.

> *"Don't be drunk with wine, because that will ruin your life. Instead, be filled with the Holy Spirit"* (Eph. 5:18, NLT).

Paul encourages us to be filled with the Spirit instead of alcohol. When filled with the Spirit, we don't have to be afraid because God did not give us a Spirit of fear.

So, what if you received a bad report from your doctor. Are you afraid? Not if you are living under the influence. You can still smile because your life has been filled to the brim with His Spirit. Being filled with the Spirit has made a huge difference in my life. Instead of being weak, I am strong. Instead of constantly struggling, I have strength for the journey ahead.

15

Taking Pain into His Presence

If you've been going through life carrying a heavy load and dragging your pain, you know it travels with you to work, shopping, and church, everywhere. You've most likely used different methods to try numbing it, such as food, achievements, drugs, alcohol, etc., only to find out these things provide temporary relief.

I know a place where we can take our pain to achieve lasting positive results. When we enter into His presence with pain, He will enter our lives with His love, peace, and healing power. God stands ready to meet with us and make us whole again.

A Mandatory Meeting

Mandatory work meetings seem to be getting longer and more frequent. Yet fewer positive outcomes occur because people are frustrated with so many meetings. But daily mandatory meetings with God enrich our lives and serve as our life lines. His presence gives us fresh air for breathing, relief for pain, and power for living. God gives us a mandate, to "come away my beloved and make spending time with me your number one priority." Without meeting with God on a regular basis, my life would not stand a chance. I would be just like a fish out of water, spiritually dead.

Since I've been in desperate need of healing, daily meetings with God have healed my heart from past pains. Meeting with God regularly also directs me on important decisions such as whom to marry and where to live. Prior to communicating with God daily, I went down a number of dead-end streets. I received prayers and words of encouragement from others, but it came a point where I had to leave the world and seek God's direction. When I did, I discovered He had been waiting for me to stop depending on others and worldly solutions and to come to Him for myself.

> *"Come unto me, all ye that labour and are heavy laden, and I will give you rest" (Matt. 11:28).*

From the beginning of time, God has been in relationship with man. Just like He watched over Adam and Eve, even after they sinned (book of Genesis), He watches over us. After Adam and Eve had eaten the forbidden fruit, they realized they were naked. God already knew but waited for them to tell Him. Then, He made them clothing from animal skins. In the same way, God wants us to come so He can cover us.

I am glad He invited me to meet with Him. For I couldn't stay in my broken condition any longer. My encounter with God was long overdue. I had been hurting far too long. He wants to meet with you too. All you have to do is accept His meeting invitation and show up. It's time to stop running to others and meet with your Daddy God.

Painful Worship

There are a lot of beautiful worship songs about pain and suffering. Songs like "His Eye is on the Sparrow," "Near the Cross," and "Amazing Grace" have provided weary people with declarations of faith in the midst of pain. We should not only experience worship when we celebrate, but also during suffering. Worship isn't a place to forget our circumstances, rather a place to bring them.

At first, I had trouble understanding the concept of worshiping while in pain. I didn't mind talking about pain but worshiping in the midst of it didn't register with me.

I figured why worship when my heart was broken? More so, how could I worship when my heart was broken? But then God showed me. Though not easy, I learned how to worship when darkness shadowed my life and hope seemed all but gone.

I remember sitting in worship services where I felt like running out the back door because I hurt so bad. I remember lying on the office floor crying to God because I was at such a low place in my life. The pain kept me going back, asking, and pleading to God for the same thing. I realized only God could help me. Even when I didn't have the strength to raise my hands or pray one word, I kept going before the Lord. I listened and sang to my favorite worship songs and worshipped in prayer.

When broken, the only thing left for me to do was worship. For I knew if I didn't give up, He would answer me. Jesus gives us a great parable of how we should always pray and not give up.

> *Saying, there was in a city a judge, which feared not God, neither regarded man: And there was a widow in that city; and she came unto him, saying, avenge me of mine adversary. And he would not for a while: but afterward he said within himself, though I fear not God, nor regard man; Yet because this widow troubleth me, I will avenge her, lest by her continual coming she weary me. (Luke 18:2–5).*

In this parable, the judge finally granted the widow woman her request because she wore him out by her continual pleading. When life hurts and doesn't make sense, I have a habit of running into the presence of God. Even when I don't know what to say, God handles my silence. When I don't understand, He can handle my confusion. It may not make sense, but to worship in painful times brings life.

When there seems to be no hope and all has been taken away, worship. Worship Him from the pain, through the pain, and with the pain. It helps bring you through it, and God will honor you for it.

Soar like an Eagle

Have you ever accepted defeat because you didn't have the strength to go on? Maybe you took multivitamins and drank high protein shakes, yet you were still tired and stressed.

But the solution to your problem is not found in a pill. It's a matter of your will. At times we all become fatigued and know how it feels to not have strength. During illness, pain, crises, and other challenges, we feel tired and defeated. But our strength can be renewed.

Many times, I didn't think I could take another step, much less get through the day. When I carried burdens threatening to defeat me, I found myself emotionally and physically spent. I couldn't see a way out. Being weak and not able to do anything about it put me in a vulnerable place. All I could do was worship and remain in His presence. So, when I came across Isaiah's account of waiting on God and mounting up as wings of eagles, my expectations grew high.

> *He giveth power to the faint; and to them that have no might he increaseth strength. Even the youths shall faint and be weary, and the young men shall utterly fall: But they that wait upon the LORD shall renew their strength; they shall mount up with wings as eagles; they shall run, and not be weary; and they shall walk, and not faint. (Isa. 40:29–31).*

Through the pains of life, I have waited on the Lord. Even if I had reached rock bottom, I came up soaring like an eagle. Renewing my strength happened much easier than I thought. I didn't have to take a pill or anything—all I had to do was wait on the Lord. We don't have to do something complicated when we hurt and can't find our way. We just have to get in His presence. For when our strength is gone, He provides the substance to go on.

When an eagle rises above the storm, he has overcome it. Like the eagle, we do not have to let life's challenges overtake us. We can allow God's strength to lift us above them. Waiting in God's presence gives us strength to soar high above life's challenges with ease, out of danger's reach. Our vantage point sees high above the storm and beyond our circumstances.

Be Still and Know

One of the main problems we encounter when entering into God's presence is getting rid of all the day's clutter and calming ourselves down. God wants to speak to us, but He doesn't like to compete with the many voices going on around us. We ask God for everything, but we don't always stop to listen to what He wants to say. A cup will never be filled if it spins on the table. In the same way, we have to cease from our busy lives if we want God's presence to flow into us.

When the world asks me to be busy, God wants me to be silent. I used to be intimidated by silence. I thought I needed to be saying something or doing something every time I went to worship God. It's okay to be silent before Him. For it was in the silence where God spoke, and I could hear Him clearly. God was not in the strong wind, nor the hurricane forces which brought floods, nor the earthquakes which caused landslides. He was not in the fire which spread across the lands and caused the sky to fill with smoke. Instead, He was found in the still small voice of my quiet time with Him. I had to be still.

"Be still and know that I am God . . ." (Ps. 46:10).

Now, regardless of what I face, I can be still in God's presence. When my body wretches with pain, I can be still and know He is God. I can't allow life to compel me to forget about God.

What about you? Have you allowed life to cause you to forget He is God? Are you burdened and drowning in despair because you forgot He is God?

When the pain closes in on us, we can find a place of solitude in God. When our life stirs in an uproar, there's a gentle, quiet place in God's presence. When our enemies make noise, boast, fume, and fight, we have no need for alarm. No matter how bad things look, God is our refuge.

Calling on God

How many times have you heard, "Call if you need anything" or "Call me and we'll do lunch." Maybe you have said them yourself. I know I have. These words have become so common place. We barely think about them. Some people mean well, and others may have never intended to call, but regardless of intent, at the end of the day, they don't. Thankfully, when God says to call Him, He means it. In fact, He waits to hear from us.

Isn't that amazing? God cares about us and is never too busy to help when we call upon Him.

Even when my pain resulted from my own doing, God never turned His back on me. He made it easy for me to call upon Him. All I had to do was open up my mouth and whisper a plea. Just one call away, He always listened to my every prayer and concern.

Yet, so often I have done everything but call on God. I worried and fretted, trying to figure out how I was going to get out of trouble. But this is not what King David did when he found himself in trouble.

"And call upon me in the day of trouble: I will deliver thee, and thou shalt glorify me" (Ps. 50:15).

Some of King David's difficulties came from his own doing, but he still called on God in his day of trouble. God doesn't distinguish His children by troublemakers and those dealing with troubles caused by someone else. He loves us no matter what. God can save us from trouble, and He never meant for us to handle it by ourselves. He is waiting on us to get off the phone and go to the throne. He said to call on Him, He will deliver us, and take us through safely to the other side.

Rest for the Soul

I don't know anyone who gets enough rest anymore. Life goes at such a fast pace. Everybody wants everything instantly, and there's no escape from life's demands. More and more stores stay open twenty-four hours a day. Online customer service and technical support hardly ever shut down. Nothing stops. We just keep going, but God wants us to rest. Pain causes fatigue, doubt, and fears. We need to rest, be refreshed, and be restored. Sometimes, we drive ourselves to the point of illness, when we have no choice but to rest.

One time I needed a place where I could go and rest. Weak and struggling, I hurt from people attacking me, so I sought a quiet resting place. I thought vacation would provide the perfect solution, but I learned differently. After working overtime to prepare and putting in more hours to catch up from being gone, the vacation caused even greater fatigue. I recognized the key to genuine rest is not discovered on a vacation. For this is only physical rest and not nearly enough.

When Jesus said come to me, He spoke about soul rest.

> *"Come unto me, all ye that labour and are heavy laden, and I will give you rest. Take my yoke upon you and learn of me; for I am meek and lowly in heart: and ye shall find rest unto your souls" (Matt. 11:28–29).*

True rest can only be found in God's presence. We can't find it in recreation, entertainment, or watching our favorite sports teams. In fact, when our teams lose, the little rest we thought we had may go away for a while. Soul rest is only given to those who come to Jesus for it. Rest for our souls comes and abides with us because of our personal relationships with God. This should be a great motivator for us to go to God and to spend time in His presence. In doing so, you will find a place of rest deeper than you have ever known.

I want to encourage you to be with the Lord and to rest in Him. For resting in His presence is a time to hear from God. It doesn't have to be for long hours. Even a brief period in His presence can fill your soul. Make a commitment to go before the Lord and just rest. Your soul needs it.

A Cry of Desperation

In life, we all walk down dark paths at times. We realize we are not brave enough or strong enough to handle life's hurts. Sometimes the pain gets so bad, we can't ignore it any longer and cry out in desperation. When doing so, we feel out of control, with no solution.

At one point in my life, I had reached a point of hopelessness in what looked like a dead-end situation. I was willing to do just about anything. In desperation, I turned completely to the Lord with uplifted hands.

As a mother knows the cry of her child, the Lord knows when we really need help. In my distress and despair, I cried out to God. His faithfulness came through, and He responded to my cry.

Blind Bartimaeus also cried out to God during his hopeless situation.

> *And they came to Jericho: and as he went out of Jericho with his disciples and a great number of people, blind Bartimaeus, the son of Timaeus, sat by the highway side begging. And when he heard that it was Jesus of Nazareth, he began to cry out, and say, Jesus, thou Sons of David, have mercy on me. And many charged him that he should hold his peace: but he cried the more a great deal, Thou Sons of David, have mercy on me. And Jesus stood still and commanded him to be called. And they call the blind man, saying unto him, be of good comfort, rise; he calleth thee. And he,*

casting away his garment, rose, and came to Jesus. And Jesus answered and said unto him, what wilt thou that I should do unto thee? The blind man said unto him, Lord, that I might receive my sight. And Jesus said unto him, go thy way; thy faith hath made thee whole. And immediately he received his sight and followed Jesus in the way. (Mark 10:46–52).

When Blind Bartimaeus heard Jesus was in the area, he began to cry out. The people told him to be quiet, but he kept crying out, louder and more persistent than before. Nothing can stop a passionate seeker who knows God and what He can do. Desperate for his sight, others' opinions didn't bother blind Bartimaeus. He kept crying out and crying out until his voice reached Jesus. Jesus responded, and Bartimaeus left there seeing. Desperately crying out to God gets His attention.

What needs press on your heart today? Cry out to God. Lean on Him completely. On call twenty-four hours a day, He specializes in emergency rescue.

The Healing Power of Worship

So many of us get caught up in an inner struggle. We don't realize in order to become the person God wants us to be we must stop fighting ourselves and surrender to God. Our healing starts by spending time with the Lord. When we get alone with Him, He comes in and touches us with His healing power. Worship brings the healing power of God into the midst of our situations. For there's no greater means for His presence to manifest than through worship.

Worship has been one of the most powerful weapons God has given me to prevail over pain and depression. I didn't notice anything when I initially started worshiping. But as time went by, I started feeling better, little by little and day by day. For when I worshipped God, He came down to be with me. Whatever was not right, He fixed it, broken pieces and all. He brought me life. I felt the warmth of His embrace as I basked in His presence.

Worship brings healing and breakthrough in our lives when we learn to praise God despite what we face. There is also Scriptural evidence of praise and worship creating an environment for healing.

> *Let our lord now command thy servants, which are before thee, to seek out a man, who is a cunning player on an harp: and it shall come to pass, when the evil spirit from God is upon thee, that he shall play with his hand, and thou shalt be well . . . And it came to pass, when the evil spirit from God was upon Saul, that David took an harp, and played with his hand: so Saul was refreshed, and was well, and the evil spirit departed from him. (1 Sam. 16:16, 23).*

Distressed by an evil spirit, King Saul called for David to play so he could be delivered from oppression. David's worship invoked God's presence and delivered King Saul from the troubling spirit. The spirit departed from him, and he was refreshed. We, too, can be delivered from the enemy's oppression through worship. When our prayers seem fruitless and we need a breakthrough, we can be healed and delivered by worshipping God. A powerful force, worship brings healing to the body, mind, and spirit.

Fill My Cup, Lord

Have you ever been thirsty for God? Do you ever long for His presence? Thirsting for God means more than a causal pick-me-up, it's a desire to spend more time in His presence drinking His unlimited supply. We can't afford to settle for a little cup every now and then. We can't continue going through the motions. We have to become serious and allow God to fill our cups and saturate those empty places in our hearts.

I have wasted so much time searching for things I thought would meet my needs. I filled my cup with possessions, positions, and other things in an effort to quench my thirst. *If I only had this or that, I could make it.* But no matter how much I did or obtained, it was not enough, and I still looked for more. I realized Jesus had created a longing and desire in me to draw closer to Him, for He is the only one who can heal my soul. I suffered from spiritual thirst and dehydration. Somehow, I knew if I didn't drink of Him, I was not going to make it. I had to experience the living water and allow Jesus to rescue me and fill my cup.

He also came to the aid of the woman at the well and satisfied a deep thirst in her heart and soul.

> *There cometh a woman of Samaria to draw water: Jesus saith unto her, Give me to drink. (For his disciples were gone away unto the city to buy meat.) Then saith the woman of Samaria unto him, how is it that thou, being a Jew, askest drink of me, which am a woman of Samaria? For the Jews have no dealings with the Samaritans. Jesus answered and said unto her, if thou knewest the gift of God, and who it is that saith to thee, give me to drink; thou wouldest have asked of him, and he would have given thee living water. The woman saith unto him, Sir, thou hast nothing to draw with, and the well is deep: from whence then hast thou that living water? Art thou greater than our father Jacob, which gave us the well, and drank thereof himself, and His children, and His cattle? Jesus answered and said unto her, whosoever drinketh of this water shall thirst again: But whosoever drinketh of the water that I shall give him shall never thirst; but the water that I shall give him shall be in him a well of water springing up into everlasting life. (John 4:7–14).*

Every day the Samaritan woman kept going back for water, for she could never get enough. But when she met Jesus, the living water,

He told her she would never thirst again. By His Spirit, Jesus reached into the deep, dark corners of her life and quenched her thirst.

In the same way Jesus filled her, every thirst within us can be quenched. Are you ready to allow the Lord to fill your cup to overflowing? He's waiting for our hearts to become open. Our circumstances are not impossible. Therefore, I encourage you to begin a new journey today by giving God your heart and saying, "Come . . . fill my cup, Lord."

16

Heart Conditions

Everybody's heart needs ongoing care as neglect can have devastating effect on our bodies. In the same way, our spiritual hearts require care and maintenance. In the Bible, the heart generally speaks of the inner person and one's spiritual life. Like the human heart, healthy spiritual hearts are vital for us to thrive.

God has charged us with the responsibility of taking care of our hearts. For what's in our hearts will show up in our actions and the ways we live and think. When we allow negative things into our hearts, we suffer the consequences. We have to keep our hearts in good condition if we want the life of Christ to flow though us.

Spiritual Heart Disease

The flow of God's life and love determines the conditions of our spiritual health. Receiving love from God is vital for our lives, but it can easily be obstructed. Spiritual heart disease happens when the flow of God's love is blocked. When a person suffers from spiritual heart disease, she has difficulty feeling love and loving others.

The arteries of our physical hearts can become clogged with cholesterol when we eat foods high in fat. In the same way, I have suffered from spiritual heart disease when my life clogged from pain, stress, and emotional bondage. Blood carries life, and increased blood flow brings health to the body. I have been lulled into a state of numbness due to a lack of God's blood flowing into my life.

At one time, pain caused a decreased blood flow to my spiritual heart, and I began experiencing emotional fatigue. My emotional healing was blocked, and His blessings couldn't get through. Sometimes my strong emotions paralyzed me. This led to a spiritual stroke, where one half of me wanted to serve God and the other half could not respond. I had to be mindful of what went on inside me and why I did some of the things I did. Allowing those negative thoughts in my heart eventually showed up in my life. My heart needed safeguarding, as I was so easily influenced by the world around me.

Besides, as I read Proverbs, it indicated I could have a healthier heart if I kept it under closer surveillance.

> *"Keep thy heart with all diligence; for out of it are the issues of life" (Prov. 4:23).*

Scripture clearly teaches the real issues of life are spiritual and matters of our hearts. We have to be mindful and guard our hearts because we are prone to wander from God, especially when problems arise. When pain overwhelms us, it affects our hearts. But if we guard our hearts, we can keep the blood flowing freely. We all want to direct our own affairs, but when we look after our hearts by letting God in, we foster good spiritual growth and prevent spiritual heart disease from creeping in.

A Heart of Stone

Precious stones such as diamonds, rubies, sapphires, and emeralds are prized possessions in our society. But when it comes to our hearts, whether a precious or ordinary stone, we don't have room for any kind.

When pain is not removed quickly, a stone can form in the heart. My heart of stone began to form early in life. It became stony and hard from adversity, disappointments, and abuse. Cold and spiritually dead, my heart lumped like rocks. I tried warming it up when with others, but it didn't last. I couldn't receive love, and I didn't know how to love myself. I tried moving on, but life gets difficult trying to live with a stone, cold heart. Spiritually blind and deaf, I couldn't see the truth or hear God speak to me.

But God is faithful. He never gave up on me. He softened my heart and guided me through those difficulties. Now I am more of a forgiving and sensitive person.

"For God maketh my heart soft, and the Almighty troubleth me" (Job 23:16).

When our hearts have been hardened by life's circumstances and we think we're beyond repair, God can soften them. We don't have to allow the world to make us hard as rocks. God can make them flexible but resilient, so we can withstand the pressure. Soft hearts focused on God go a long way in warming up a stone-cold world.

A Broken Heart

The world is filled with sad and broken-hearted people. A preacher once said to his students, "If you preach to the broken-hearted, you will always have an audience." We live in a world filled with broken relationships, promises, and lives, as well as no confidence in the future. When sorrow reaches a level of intensity, which goes beyond our limit to handle it, the heart breaks and starts to bleed. A broken heart can be brought on by multiple causes, such as pain from a divorce, sickness, loss of job or some other loss, or emotional distress. While we may not all agree on the cause, there is one thing we all agree with . . . it hurts to have your heart broken.

I have experienced several heartbreaking circumstances with such extreme pain I wanted to grab it and pull it out. I couldn't though, because I couldn't even grasp its root issues and magnitude. I wondered if I would ever get on the other side of it.

A medical doctor can fix problems which can be seen. But what about the wounds we can't see? I couldn't tell the doctor, "I have a broken heart. Can you fix it?" Who else could I turn to? God provides healing for broken hearts where we can receive complete recovery.

King David, a man after God's own heart, endured many saddening conditions. But each time, he turned to God and recovered.

> "He healeth the broken in heart, and bindeth up their wounds" (Ps. 147:3).

A broken heart is reduced to fragments and shattered into many pieces. But God will reach down into our spirits and bandage up our wounds to stop the bleeding.

Do you feel like your heart has been reduced to fragments? If so, God can heal you. Hand Him your heart and invite Him into the broken places. He will mend your heart and put all those little pieces back together again.

Emotional Pain

We often monitor our physical health and tend to be proactive in dealing with physical pain, but rarely do we get checkups and seek help for emotional pain. In fact, pain caused by emotional distress, such as rejection, loneliness, guilt, failure, etc., can cause longer-lasting damage to our health and quality of life than physical pain. I have known people who hurt so badly emotionally, the pain made them question if life was worth living.

There have been times in my life when I was depressed and emotionally broken. After being exposed to chronic stress from trauma, rejections, and abuse, my emotional well-being spiraled downward. My pains worsened when my thoughts were consumed with harmful emotions as I replayed and relived those painful, traumatic events. The pain constantly gripped my mind. Although I tried getting rid of the thoughts so I could feel better, they crippled me emotionally and affected my mood, relationships, personal life, and career.

Emotional pain can be so devastating. It can actually cause physical pain. One day, I went to the doctor because I developed slight chest pains and felt bad. The doctor performed numerous tests to find out if something was wrong with my heart. After the testing, he found nothing. He simply advised me to go home and get some rest because I looked emotionally drained. My heart hurt so badly during those times. I didn't disclose the information to my doctor, but because I had been hurting for so long, the pain on the inside had gradually made its way to the outside.

Just as clogged arteries prevent blood from flowing freely into a physical heart, emotional pain clogged up my life and prevented the very life of God from flowing into me. I had lost my spark and energy.

It seemed like God had moved far away, but actually He was much closer than I realized.

"The LORD is close to the brokenhearted; he rescues those who spirits are crushed" (Ps. 34:18, NLT).

Our God is indeed the God of hurting hearts. Whether we realize it or not, God is closest to us when we experience pain. In today's world, people look to so many other things to heal their hurts. They turn to drugs, money, power, more stuff, more friends, and the list goes on. None of these things can take away our pain. Only God has the healing ointment.

An Ungrateful Heart

Today, being ungrateful is far too common. Children forget to thank their parents for all they do. We take for granted the ways others have helped us. Above all, we fail to thank God for His blessings. Being ungrateful starts in the heart and gradually manifests itself in our emotions, desires, thinking, and outlooks on life. It affects our relationships with God and then eventually affects all those around us.

There have been many times in my life when I was ungrateful. God taught me some painful lessons on being thankful through tough situations and circumstances. Those lessons were experienced through trials and heartaches where I learned gratitude. There have been instances when I felt life had not been fair. As I focused on the negative and not the positive, I failed to thank God for what He had already done for me. The fact of me even being alive to have those issues was a blessing all by itself.

Now as I look behind the clutter, I see God's goodness through the good and the bad. When life derailed my plans, desires, and expectations, God still led me through the circumstances. When unpleasant things happened in my life, I may not have felt thankful, yet Scripture says God wants us to be thankful in all situations.

"In everything give thanks: for this is the will of God in Christ Jesus concerning you" (1 Thess. 5:18).

Now even in the worst conditions and circumstances, I no longer have an ungrateful heart. I am thankful for how far He has brought me and everything He has taught me. I am thankful for how He led me and how He fed me. I thank God for where He brought me from and for where He is taking me.

A Proud Heart

Another serious heart condition, pride is an attitude of the heart which says life revolves around us or at least it should. As swelling poses danger to the body, so does pride in our hearts. Pride causes us to think life is all about us. A destructive behavior, pride will lead to a life of shame if we don't get rid of it.

Oftentimes, I have struggled with having a proud heart. I believed I deserved better than what life had brought me. I had my own style about doing things and would do just about anything to have my way. This sinful nature of pride, lead me to be highly independent. I felt I was self-made and didn't need anyone's help. I couldn't stand the thought of allowing other people to control me.

Having a proud heart can be painful. I struggled with selfishness, jealously, and a cold heart toward God. I appeared to be shy, but I really had a desire to be noticed. And when I didn't get the attention I thought I deserved, I became sad and disappointed, sometimes angry. I continued along this destructive path until God brought me down. He would not tolerate my pride any longer. He stepped in and saved me from myself.

> *"Likewise, ye younger, submit yourselves unto the elder. Yea, all of you be subject one to another, and be clothed with humility: for God resisteth the proud, and giveth grace to the humble" (1 Pet. 5:5).*

God gives favor to the humble, but He will not tolerate a proud heart. Consequently, God will not allow the prideful to prosper in life. God would no longer put up with my prideful thinking that everything had to revolve around me. Pride will bring us to dishonor, which is the last thing a prideful person wants. When I wanted to go high, I went low. I had to fight pride on my knees if I wanted to keep it at bay. Nothing in this life is all about me—it is all about Jesus and Him only.

A Heart Transplant

Most of us will agree we have some matters of the heart we would like to change. Our hearts are like a house. A house sometimes only needs a little repair, such as replacing cracked windows and putting on a fresh coat of paint. But oftentimes, a house requires major renovations. Some of our hearts are too far gone ever to be mended. They have suffered significant damage and appear close to collapsing. God knows minor repairs won't last. Instead, He wants to tear the whole thing down and build a new one. He wants to transform us from the inside out.

When we make poor decisions and don't do things the godly way, it affects our hearts. When prideful, my heart filled with things which kept me from having a close relationship with God. I desperately needed help and wanted to change, but I struggled to find solutions. Self-help books and CDs weren't working. No matter how hard I tried, I couldn't cure my problem, nor could I escape the real me on the inside.

One day when alone with God and frantically looking for answers, I had a vision. Profound, the image left a lasting impression. The vision showed a picture of a hand coming out of the clouds carrying a bright-red heart. This heart slowly came toward me and entered my chest. When the hand left my chest, it no longer held the red heart, but it carried a black rock. I stood amazed of what I had witnessed and pondered its meaning. In an effort to understand, I sought God about the vision. He led me to a Scripture in the Bible which describes exactly what I envisioned.

> *"And I will give them one heart, and I will put a new spirit within you; and I will take the stony heart out of their flesh, and will give them an heart of flesh"* (Ezek. 11:19).

My problem signaled danger, and I had only one hope. I needed a heart transplant. I needed my old heart removed and replaced with a new living, beating heart. And that's what God promises in Ezekiel, not to just wipe our slates clean from past hurts and pains, but to give us a heart transplant.

There is hope for those who sincerely desire to change. This hope starts with admitting we can't change on our own. We can't make ourselves new hearts. Medical science is good, but it's not that good. Deeply wounded hearts require a gifted hand. And lasting change requires the help of a skillful surgeon, the Lord. He wants to remove our old hearts of stone and replace them with hearts of flesh which beat with the cleansing life blood of Jesus.

17

Covered with Guilt and Shame

There's always something to feel guilty about. People feel guilty for not remembering their spouses' birthdays, for cutting corners at work or for skipping church on Sunday. Sometimes after eating too much chocolate my conscious screams, "Guilty, guilty, guilty!"

Guilt is an emotional distress which leaves a person blaming herself for something she feels she may have done wrong and regrets. Guilt feelings also exist when someone perceives she has fallen short of self-expectations or the expectations of others. A person who feels guilty typically reflects on what she should have or could have done differently.

While guilt takes place when a person realizes what she has done was wrong, shame on the other hand, is a painful feeling generated by a combination of wrongdoing and how the person judges herself. When someone feels embarrassed or disgraced, she feels shame and sees herself as a stain or a bad mark to others. It's as if her troubles strut around on stage for all to see.

A lot of people spend a great deal of time covered with guilt and shame, and it's important to deal with these painful emotions in order to lead a more peaceful and satisfying life.

The hurts and pain I brought on myself caused a lot of guilt feelings. The things I regretted doing in the past created a lot of discomfort. Guilty feelings kept me from enjoying life, so I had to learn how to get out from under the stain of guilt if I wanted to be happy.

A Guilt Trip

If we do not learn how to deal with guilt the right way, we end up going on a guilt trip, which leads to discouragement, shame, and depression, just to name a few. Traveling through life with guilt does not lead to happy traveling, and more importantly, goes against God's will for our lives.

People will say and do things which can cause us to react in the wrong way. For instance, I had people place false guilt upon me by blaming me for their problems. Though innocent, I ended up acting like a guilty person. Some people love to take others on a guilt trip where they can lay a heavy load of guilt on someone besides themselves. I took myself guilt tripping as I struggled to forgive myself for past sins, failures, and mistakes.

When I discovered the following Scripture, I even felt guilty for heaping guilt on myself! But, according to Micah, my sins and past failures had already been dealt with.

> *"He will turn again, he will have compassion upon us; he will subdue our iniquities; and thou wilt cast all their sins into the depths of the sea" (Micah 7:19).*

Finally, I overcame guilt by not focusing on past failures, which had clearly been washed away and no longer existed. I realized no one could take me on a guilt trip if I wasn't willing to pack my bags and take the ride. Thankfully, this Scripture encouraged me to stop focusing on what had already happened and shut out the voices of others. Their problems were not my mess, so I stopped feeling responsible for them.

Overcoming Divorce Guilt

As children, most of us desire to grow up and have a successful marriage. When the marriage unravels, we may blame ourselves for everything leading up to the end, but a lingering feeling of divorce guilt is not healthy. If we continue to feel guilty and dwell on the negative, it robs us of joy and peace.

I hated breaking my marriage vows and felt guilty for ending my marriage. I had caused a lot of pain and hurt to loved ones. Also, I put a lot of pressure on myself and felt like I had let everyone in my family down. It's normal to hurt and feel guilty when ending a marriage. I had so many guilty feelings and unanswered questions. Was I feeling guilty because of the pain? Was I guilty because I wished I could have fixed the relationship since I had invested so much time into it? I looked at the divorce with 20/20 hindsight and picked myself to pieces. But hindsight glasses don't exist, and neither should guilt. Now I realize how I did the best with what I had at the time.

> *"And ye now therefore have sorrow: but I will see*
> *you again, and your heart shall rejoice, and your joy*
> *no man taketh from you" (John 16:22).*

Yes, divorce can spark a lot of painful guilt. But I decided to not allow guilt to steal my joy any longer. I took the guilt and turned it around by accepting the divorce and forgiving my ex-spouse. This opened up a new pathway for my future.

Since I have gotten rid of those guilty feelings, my life has changed for the better. I have shifted my energy from guilt to more positive actions which have benefited me. I have found freedom, joy, purpose, and abundant life.

Is There Shame on You?

Think back to a time when you were ashamed. Perhaps you were falsely accused of cheating in school and punished unjustly. Maybe your reputation was marred, and you had to tough it out. Or you could have done something wrong, but your punishment seemed inappropriate and you have had to carry the stain of the embarrassment ever since.

Some things in my life left me feeling ashamed and devalued. The divorces I suffered, the abuse, and the effects of my past resulted in me feeling ashamed to even show my face in public sometimes. My loss of dignity and the damage I endured tempted me to doubt God's ability to restore me from those shameful situations. But in Scripture, God encourages all who have been shamed in childhood or adulthood.

> *"Fear not; for thou shalt not be ashamed: neither be thou confounded; for thou shalt not be put to shame: for thou shalt forget the shame of thy youth, and shalt not remember the reproach of thy widowhood anymore"* (Isa. 54:4).

Past experiences have their lessons, but when they weaken our present lives, it serves as painful memories. God gives us the gift of forgetfulness to take away those shameful situations. We no longer need to be shamed by our pasts. For God will increase us and cause us to forget those circumstances which brought feelings of embarrassment and humiliation. Our futures will be so great, and we can rejoice because we have forgotten our shame and remembered the reproach no more.

No Shame on You

Many of us struggle with painful feelings of shame and condemnation. Condemnation can be brought upon us by sinning, losing the trust of others, or by hurting others. When we hurt someone or have been injured ourselves and have not forgiven, we walk in guilt, shame, and condemnation. Painful memories of past experiences can torment us night and day. Condemning thoughts can lead to feelings of self-harm, harming someone else, or turning to alcohol and drugs to ease the pain.

I have been a Christian for a long time, but as a Christian, I have sinned and have not always done the right thing. I still have to apologize and repent to God. But after repentance, I wondered why I sometimes still felt condemned.

Feeling condemned led me to evaluate the nature of Satan. The truth is Satan attacked me with the feeling of condemnation to remind me of how badly I messed up. He wanted me to believe God was not going to help me get out of my troubles and pain. He wanted me to accept the lie that God was no longer thrilled with me as He once was. But God knows I am human and can stumble no matter how hard I strive. This is why He sent Jesus, not to inflict condemnation but to bring freedom from shame. Jesus demonstrated this when dealing with a woman caught in the very act of adultery.

> *And the scribes and Pharisees brought unto him a woman taken in adultery; and when they had set her in the midst. They say unto him, Master, this woman was taken in adultery, in the very act. Now Moses in the law commanded us, that such should be stoned: but what sayest thou? This they said, tempting him, that they might have to accuse him. But Jesus stooped down, and with his finger wrote on the ground, as though he heard them not. So when they continued asking him, he lifted up himself, and said unto them, He that is without sin among you, let him first cast a stone at her. And again he stooped down and wrote on the ground. And they which heard it, being convicted by their own conscience, went out one by one, beginning at the eldest, even unto the last: and Jesus was left alone, and the woman standing in the midst. When Jesus had lifted up himself, and saw none but the woman, he said unto her, Woman, where are those thine accusers? Hath no man condemned thee? She said, No man, LORD.*

And Jesus said unto her, neither do I condemn thee: go, and sin no more. (John 8:3–11).

Guilty of adultery, this woman also suffered public shame by her accusers. But Jesus didn't accuse, He forgave her. This is a perfect picture of God's merciful heart toward us in our battles with sin and shame. The way He handled this woman depicts the same way He would handle you and me if we were caught in the same situation. Instead of saying, "Shame on you," Jesus chose to say to us what He said to this hurting, embarrassed woman. "No shame on you."

God Made Me Clean

Satan wants us to feel damaged and dirty. He loves to pour guilt and shame on us and cover us in condemnation. He strives toward having us hang our heads and hide ourselves from God. But we don't have to hide. Instead, we can go to God and allow Him to purify us from the stain of guilt and shame.

I felt I had made a mess of my life. I made some terrible decisions and knowingly went down the wrong path. I have sinned in some bad ways and thought God could never love me or do anything through me. Covered in guilt and shame, I needed something to remove this dark and dim cover from my life.

"But the voice spoke again: 'Do not call something unclean if God has made it clean'" (Acts 10:15, NLT).

When I thought my filthy life piled up too high, Jesus came and made it clean. I tried hiding the stains of my dirty laundry, yet even then God came along and removed every blemish and spot. Though powerful emotions, guilt and shame will never be more powerful than God's grace.

You may not be able to see this type of cleansing in the mirror, for our God is the inside God. He has cleansed and removed all those things which tainted my life, and I know He can do the same for you.

The cleansing power of God has dissolved all the guilt and shame. Be encouraged. The God who forgave me will forgive you. The God who changed me will change you. The God who cleansed me will clean you.

From Shame to Significance

No matter what causes our shame, whether filing for bankruptcy, struggling with an addiction, or making a mistake, God wants to help us overcome shame, so we can fulfill His purpose in our lives. We have to make a crucial decision and choose between allowing shame to rob us of our faith in God and doing whatever it takes to turn our lives around.

If you are tired of wasting your life living in shame, God's healing power can bring you from a place of shame to a place of significance.

I felt ashamed of things my family had done. I felt embarrassed when in public, especially at school and social events. Although I grew up in a dysfunctional family, I decided to surrender the situation to God. Realizing He was able to redeem my past and guide me into a better future, I turned from those debilitating thoughts and liberated myself to embrace the life God had for me, free from shame. When I thought my past had disqualified me, I learned to take courage and be empowered by looking at the life of Ruth. Ruth left Moab and went to Bethlehem where she moved from shame to significance.

> *"And Salmon begat Booz of Rahab; and Booz begat Obed of Ruth; and Obed begat Jesse; And Jesse begat David the king; and David the king begat Solomon of her that had been the wife of Urias" (Matt. 1:5–6).*

It is truly profound to see Ruth's name, a Gentile woman from the land of Moab, end up in the lineage of Jesus Christ. Moabite people were cut off from God due to their incestuous relationships. Ruth must have felt a deep sense of rejection and shame. But she persevered when she had many strikes against her. Perhaps you have been like Ruth, shameful of things your family has done. But it doesn't matter how many strikes you have against you. For if God is with you, He will not allow you to strike out in life. If He did it for Ruth, He can do it for you. You can walk away from your shameful past today. Leave the shame and walk over to a place of significance.

A Season of Double

For everyone who has been ashamed or disgraced in some way, this can be your time to receive a double blessing in your life. You may have been through shameful times, but today you can walk into a new season.

Incidents and painful memories from the past can carry great waves of shame. These memories can occur repeatedly with powerful feelings each time. There have been times when people mocked me because I didn't have something, or I was not at a particular level in my life. But God did not allow them to have the final say or the last word. God has opened double doors in my life. He has gone before me to make the crooked places straight and the rough places smooth. Because of the shame I endured, the insults, and the constant put-downs, God paved the way for me to receive a double pay.

> *"For your shame ye shall have double; and for confusion they shall rejoice in their portion: therefore, in their land they shall possess the double: everlasting joy shall be unto them"* (Isa. 61:7).

Here in Isaiah, God says He will give us twice as much in blessings after going through shame, hurts, and disappointments. Indeed, this can be a season of double for those who have passed the test of time, pursuing God in spite of the shame they carried. God is good in every situation, and we can live our lives and fulfill our destinies. Though it may seem we are losing out, in the end, we can receive a double portion. God does not want any of us to end up in shame. For we are not destined for shame, but for double blessings and double honor in life.

18

From Trauma to Triumph

Traumatic events flood our daily news feeds. School shootings, bullying, wars, terrorism, natural disasters, sexual harassment, the list goes on. While these events may not directly affect us, personal everyday traumas do. Perhaps a friend commits suicide, a woman you know gets battered and raped, a child suffers from abuse, or a serious accident leaves you in unbearable pain. These types of trauma are equally sad and heart-wrenching although they may never make national news.

Trauma inflicts a strong emotional response to a distressing event. It shatters our sense of security and leaves us in a state of shock. Trauma overwhelms the ability to cope and can torment us for the rest of our lives. But there is help in recovering from trauma, whether it was a few days ago or a few decades ago. We may have gone through traumatic experiences, but we don't have to stay there. God can deliver us.

Stuck at the Trauma Center

When confronted with dangers, our bodies respond by giving us energy to either fight or escape the threats. But when the threats overwhelm us, we naturally freeze. Trauma victims struggle with painful emotions and frightening memories that recur over and over again. It's like their brains freeze in time.

When I walked away from abusive and harmful situations, I thought they would no longer have a negative impact on me. But I soon discovered although no longer in those situations, the impact they had embedded in my soul. Escaping the emotional stress seemed impossible. Stuck in trauma mode, I couldn't release the grip that horrific events had on me. It influenced how I saw myself and the world, as well as how I reacted to situations and related to other people.

Being stuck in trauma mode reminds me of living on a dirt road in the country. When it rains, the road becomes a muddy mess. Sometimes a vehicle gets stuck in the mud and can't break free. The wheels spin fast, but the car can't move. Someone has to come along and push it out of the mud, or the tires have to somehow gain traction. This situation illustrates how God will rescue us from situations which hold us captive, either push us out or give us something to grip.

*"For I the LORD thy God will hold thy right hand,
saying unto thee, fear not; I will help thee" (Isa. 41:13).*

Do you have traumatic pictures continually play in your mind? Are you stuck in the past trauma of a horrible experience or accident? Though it may seem impossible, you can overcome its paralyzing hold on your life. Yes, it happened, but it doesn't have to keep you from moving forward. God wants to help. He doesn't want you to be stuck in trauma mode the rest of your life. The trauma came to past. It didn't come to stay. Take God by the hand and allow Him to pull you out of the rut. He will give you the traction you need to start a new course in life. He will heal you and put your trauma behind you where it belongs.

The Home Fire

I was thirteen years old when we lost our home in a fire. I still remember the dreadful day. I got the horrible news while taking a math test at school. My teacher said I could finish the test later, so

179

I left school and rushed to be with my family. On the way home, I hoped everybody was wrong, but as we drove closer, I saw large balls of black smoke billow in the sky. When we arrived, I saw only ashes where our home had once sat.

Witnessing our home burn traumatized me. Afterward, I encountered all sorts of sounds, smells, and feelings, which reminded me of the fire and all I had lost. I didn't just lose my house in the fire, but sentimental and cherished items such as family photos, my track and field trophies, ribbons, and clothing. While grateful no one was harmed, I was heart-broken by losing my personal items.

I struggled to handle the trauma and make sense out of it. While family and friends helped us, no amount of sympathy and material items could ease the pain. And conversations about the fire only led to recurring images and thoughts about the disaster. It caused a lot of anxiety, nervous disorder, and many sleepless nights. I would just lie in bed, staring at the ceiling, wondering if I would ever get over the pain and loss.

The physical and emotional recovery took a while, but with emotional support and help from family, friends, church members, and others, I gradually picked up the pieces of my shattered life and found ways to keep on living. God eased my fears and provided for me when I greatly needed it.

> *"And I will restore to you the years that the locust hath eaten, the cankerworm, and the caterpillar, and the palmerworm, my great army which I sent among you" (Joel 2:25).*

With my childhood home destroyed, I lost my sense of security. Slowly, I found a place of safety in God's arms. God has more than restored what I lost in the fire, He made it better. God gave us a better home, and I ended up with more than I ever had before. What I lost in the fire was nothing compared to what I gained.

If you're going through a similar period of loss, it's only for a season. God has beautiful plans for you and will restore what's been lost. That's the kind of Father He is.

A Bruised Peach

Physical abuse and domestic violence are an unfortunate reality in today's world. The bruising and the breaking which occurs can leave many lasting effects, both physical and emotional. Physical abuse can lead to trauma with serious injuries, leaving the victims feeling embarrassed, devalued, and unwanted like a bruised peach.

Typically, abuse makes a person become silent, feel inferior, and fearful. When I suffered abuse, I withdrew from others, felt worthless, and feared confronting the harmful behavior. I wondered how I could love someone who treated me so badly. Painful both physically and emotionally, the abuse hurt the most when the person who made me feel loved one day, made me feel unloved the next. Physical abuse devastated me as the visible and invisible wounds made it difficult to cope. The aftermath of the emotional and physical abuse left me with many raw emotions and open wounds. I felt like a bruised peach, damaged and worthless. Initially, I didn't seek help because I wondered if anyone understood my pain. But Jesus knew my pain, for He, too, was bruised.

> *"But he was wounded for our transgressions, he was bruised for our iniquities: the chastisement of our peace was upon him; and with his stripes we are healed" (Isa. 53:5).*

When people hurt, they often refuse help, saying no one knows their stories. Although some folks haven't experienced similar pain, Jesus has. Bruised and battered, Jesus relentlessly pursued His ultimate purpose, to save the world from sin.

Peaches are delicate fruit which can easily bruise. They may appear rotten, but they are not. They just have been bruised and handled in a rough way. Maybe a few spots need to be cut out, but they still have a purpose.

When people are bruised and abused, they think God can't use them because their wounds show. But the truth is, although bruised on the outside, they still have purpose on the inside.

Have you been bruised and battered? Don't conceal the bruises any longer. Reveal them to God so He can heal them. He can turn your bruises into a blessing.

Facing the Fear

People have numerous reasons to be afraid. Lack of experience, fear of the unknown, fear of heights, etc., all stir up fear. While all of these may be real, trauma triggers fear to shoot off the scale. It can rock worlds. But as overwhelming as fear may be, trauma victims have to eventually face it. After all, fears often have a way of showing back up sooner or later until they're dealt with.

Why did I feel scared even when I was not in danger? Fear haunted me for years. I knew what was happening, but I couldn't seem to stop it. My brain constantly sensed danger. I wondered if my brain learned fear from trauma, then could I possibly help my brain change again. I didn't want to face my past, but I refused to live in fear for the rest of my life. I wanted to try and deal with it one more time, hoping this time, it would be different. I decided if I wanted to get rid of those feelings of fear and regain victory over my life, I had to deal with them like King David did.

> *"And it came to pass, when the Philistine arose, and came and drew nigh to meet David, that David hasted, and ran toward the army to meet the Philistine"* (1 Sam. 17:48).

David was a warrior, and this Scripture shows how he dealt with troubles in life. When faced with challenges, David didn't run from them. In First Samuel, he ran to the battlefront and faced the Philistines. By his example, God showed me I couldn't afford to waste any more time sitting on life's sidelines. I had to get in the game and confront my fears to have some peace. While facing our fears can be uncomfortable at best, avoiding the situation only makes it worst.

Through God's strength, I chose to face my fear, stand my ground, and make my situation better.

The very thing you fear the most is the very thing God wants you to attack and overcome. Beginning now, I encourage you to square up your shoulders and look fear in the face. Give it a deadly blow and command it to leave once and for all.

Feeling Safe in an Unsafe World

In an increasingly unsafe world, people seek safety and security. Locally and worldwide, we face safety threats every day. Despite household security features and national security measures, we're still afraid.

Trauma left me feeling jumpy, nervous, and overly sensitive to just about anything. My trust had been stolen, and I saw the world as a dangerous place. I struggled with the possibility of actually enjoying life, lacking confidence things would ever work out. Constantly I looked over my shoulders and wondered when the next disaster would strike. It was hard for me to rest and have peace in the world. But Scripture told me God wants me to be safe, that He had an answer for my security concerns.

> *"He that dwelleth in the secret place of the most High shall abide under the shadow of the Almighty"*
> *(Ps. 91:1).*

As reflected in the above Scripture, the Lord provides security and protection for those who put their trust in Him and make Him their refuge. We can be safe living under God's very own shadow. When we abide in the secret place, we live with God in the same house, under the same roof. We can't get any closer.

God has a security system which actually works and brings peace. Now I am safe and secure, living with God while here on earth. I no longer live in a state of insecurity, rather in the Lord's house, under His covering.

Unpleasant Memories

While full of many wonderful memories, life can bring painful and frustrating moments. Recurrent bad memories are a horrible thing to experience. Living through a traumatic experience creates enough challenges, but having to relive them countless times as they play over and over in your mind produces torment.

The memories of my traumatic experiences were hard for me to shake. I felt as if the images stayed glued to my brain, stuck in the corners of my mind. I wondered why God didn't intervene and take those bad memories from me sooner.

While I would have probably been better off not remembering and reliving some experiences, I needed to go back mentally to a place where I became stuck and resolve the situation, so I could move forward. Though not easy, I brought back the memories of my painful past and changed the way I looked at them. In doing so, I changed my perception, putting a positive spin on even my worst memories. This process neutralized the harmful effects from my past by taking the sting away and healing my emotional scars.

Bad memories can be terrible, but they can also be of help. Determined to not allow those painful experiences happen to me again, my bad memories have caused me to develop a deep hatred for trauma and a passion for abused and battered women. Those unpleasant memories have inspired me to help others struggling with the same horrific difficulties which once had me bound.

Time Heals Nothing

Have you ever gone through a bad situation and someone told you it would get better, just give it time? One day, I overheard someone say, "Time heals all wounds." I just wanted to scream. If you have suffered trauma in your past and you haven't sought healing, chances are you still deal with the effects of it, regardless of how long ago it happened.

The passing of time did not promote my healing. The pain just continued. I got by for a while dealing with my past. But after a while, I found myself asking, "Where did that come from?' and "Why did I react in such a horrible way?" Time is not a magical wound eraser. Years, months, and weeks went by, and my pain still lingered. The hurt didn't go away no matter what the calendar said. Time didn't have the power to heal me, only God did.

> *"For I will restore health unto thee, and I will heal thee of thy wounds, saith the LORD; because they called thee an Outcast, saying, this is Zion, whom no man seeketh after" (Jer. 30:17).*

You may have been dealing with trauma for many years, but God can heal you today. Don't wait any longer on time to heal you. It will only magnify the pain and delay your healing. Allow God to heal you and turn your trauma into a source of blessing in your life and in the lives of others.

My Trip to the Psychiatrist

Trauma survivors can have symptoms so debilitating they interfere with daily living. I began experiencing distress through flashbacks, which made me relive the abuse and traumatic experiences all over again. I also had dreams and nightmares, which often woke me up at night, anxious and afraid. I suffered with these symptoms for years and didn't want to talk to anyone about them. After struggling, I finally consulted a psychiatrist.

After sharing my past, I was diagnosed with posttraumatic stress syndrome (PTSD) and received a prescription to cope with my anxiety and to prevent feelings of fear and panic attacks. The medications probably would have helped some. But I wanted to get to the root of the problem, not cover them up. After discussing the situation with my husband, he told me, "Arvis, you don't need to take those pills, just wait on God. He's going to heal you." So I didn't take the pills, nor did I seek further treatment.

The psychiatrist expressed a desire to help me overcome my problems, for his goal was to help me "function" better. But I needed more than just "functioning," I needed healing. Although I felt bad, I didn't get ahead of myself. I waited on God's healing. My symptoms occurred less and less over the years. With God's help, I worked through my trauma issues without taking prescription medications. I was completely healed!

All I Want Is a Good Night's Sleep

Trauma survivors often struggle with simple things which others take for granted, such as a good night's sleep. For years, I had a difficult time falling and staying asleep. Flashbacks, nightmares, and troubling thoughts made it almost impossible for me to relax and stay asleep. This caused a tremendous amount of stress. I couldn't sleep no matter where I stayed … at home, a hotel, a relative or friend's house, the outcome was the same, no sleep.

Desperate to manage my anxiety and sleeping problems, I started taking pills and sedatives to help me sleep through the night. Although the pills helped some, they couldn't be a long-term solution. They triggered some weird feelings along with many other unwanted side effects. So what else could I do? Does God care if I couldn't sleep or hadn't slept well in days? When I delved into Scripture, I found God really does care and actually has a lot to say about sleep.

> *"When thou liest down, thou shalt not be afraid: yea, thou shalt lie down, and thy sleep shall be sweet" (Prov. 3:24).*

Notice the connection between anxiety, fear, and sleeplessness. Anxious thoughts and terrifying memories make it hard to sleep peacefully. Yet God says we are not to be afraid when we lie down if we want to sleep well. We are to lie down and commit ourselves into His hands and not allow distressing things to keep us up all night. Now when I read the above Scripture from Proverbs, I can be assured of sleeping in peacefulness, free from distracting cares and terrors. For I depend on God to give me undisturbed rest as I depend on Him. What better truth do I need to sleep on?

The Enemy's Plan Didn't Work

The enemy wants to ruin anything he can get his hands on. He wants to destroy our peace, joy, family, health, marriage, everything. He knows our weaknesses and understands our tendencies. He plots for us to stumble so he can ultimately destroy us. The enemy has many strategies to keep us from becoming all God intends for us to be. One of his main schemes is trauma, intended to damage and plague us for the remainder of our days.

The enemy did all he could to stop me. That's why he worked through people to try to destroy me. But now I take it as a compliment and try not to let it upset me. For Satan only attacks those worth attacking. I learned my trauma was nothing but *the reproaches against my assignment*. Satan was not after me, but my assignment. But God is just, and evil will never win. Satan's plan backfired. For a moment, things looked hopeless, I thought I would not survive, but I lived to tell about it. My traumatic experiences didn't make me weak—they did just the opposite. With God's help, they gave me resilience, determination, and strength to help me overcome. I have also been able to help others who have been through similar crises.

Have you ever gone through something which should have destroyed you, but instead, you ended up thriving in the situation? This is what happened to the children of Israel.

> *"But the more they afflicted them, the more they multiplied and grew. And they were grieved because of the children of Israel"* (Exod. 1:12).

The Egyptians thought putting the children of Israel through hard labor would weaken them. Instead, they grew stronger and multiplied. If we continue in spite of our troubles, Satan's plan will not work against us. The more he attacks us, the more we will overcome. Satan can't stop the work of God. The Lord watches over His people, and we end up growing in the dark, thriving in the very thing which should have consumed us.

19

Shaped through Suffering

We all can expect a certain degree of suffering, especially in a fallen world. Suffering is anything which causes pain or hardship. It may be caused by physical suffering to our bodies, the common pressures of life, or from the emotional struggles of dealing with anger, worry, or fear. Regardless the cause, suffering is real, inevitable, and painful.

I've been surprised at the number of trials I've experienced. Long ago, I felt I had met my quota already and it was time for pain to go and bother someone else. I had always heard suffering was good for us. This saying reminds me of cod liver oil, which may be good for me, but tough to swallow! When hurting, I took pills to ease the pain, prayed, and tried to develop a plan to avoid it. I wanted to make it go away and sometimes even wanted to erase it from the dictionary. I rarely, however, considered suffering as a part of God's plan for my life.

Suffering goes much deeper than being hurt. Often God uses suffering as a tool to make us and to shape our faith. Untrained in the ways of God and how He uses suffering to test His people, I was just a babe in Christ when my suffering started. I didn't have a lot of faith. I thought the amount of suffering I endured was abnormal. But Peter reminds us suffering is not abnormal at all.

"Beloved, think it not strange concerning the fiery trial which is to try you, as though some strange thing happened unto you" (1 Pet. 4:12).

When trials come upon us, we tend to think "Why me? What did I do wrong?" But oftentimes, trials come to test and change us. We all can expect to suffer. This is a reality we find troubling, but growth requires testing. Imagine being a college student who needs her progress measured. How can progress be measured without testing? If we take away the trials and testing, how do we measure growth? Scripture says we should not be surprised when suffering comes our way. For suffering is not a strange thing, it comes with the package.

It Will Only Hurt for a Little While

In the midst of suffering, we often wonder how much more we have to endure. While our sufferings may seem long, they are actually short compared to eternity. Looking at eternity helps us to endure suffering because we know the pain will not last forever.

As a little girl, I loved to play outside. One day as I ran barefoot over the yard, I stepped on a nail, and it went into my foot. Crying, I immediately ran into the house. After my mom pulled the nail out, she grabbed the rubbing alcohol. I said, "Mom, the alcohol will burn." She confirmed it would sting, but "only for a little while." Well, to me, a little while seemed like an eternity. But after everything was said and done, Mom proved to be right. It only hurt for a little while. I applied this principle to my troubles in life. Pain and suffering will happen, but it will end. It lasts only for a season. Scripture tells us God puts a limit on our suffering.

"But the God of all grace, who hath called us unto his eternal glory by Christ Jesus, after that ye have suffered a while, make you perfect, stablish, strengthen, settle you" (1 Pet. 5:10).

We can be encouraged today because God has stamped an expiration date on our pains and hardships. Sometimes life can leave deep wounds which sting and burn like rubbing alcohol. But remember, it will only hurt for a little while. We may have to revisit some bad things we did in our pasts, and we may have been suffering for a while. Although life has caused lots of hurts and pain, the agony is only temporary. The suffering is only for a season, and at some point, God will bring us out of it.

Leaning on God's Grace

It's good to know suffering is temporary, until God comes along to rectify the problem. But what do we do in the meantime, when the suffering has seemed to make itself at home in our lives? How do we endure the pain? Rather than praying to avoid suffering, a more effective approach might be to ask God to give us strength and supply the grace for us to persevere.

I am thankful for the grace of God working in my life. When dark seasons came about, I learned to recognize His grace, regardless of my ability to see it. When my resources were low, I leaned on God's grace, and He provided for all my needs. His grace has enabled me to carry on in spite of all the challenges. Yes, I asked God to remove the pain, but he didn't right away. Instead, He gave me His grace to endure. God will give us the grace if we were meant to experience the pain and suffering. For instance, God didn't remove Paul's source of suffering, instead He gave Him the grace to deal with it.

> *And lest I should be exalted above measure through the abundance of the revelations, there was given to me a thorn in the flesh, the messenger of Satan to buffet me, lest I should be exalted above measure. For this thing I besought the Lord thrice, that it might depart from me. And he said unto me, my grace is sufficient for thee: for my strength is made perfect in weakness. Most gladly therefore will I rather glory*

*in my infirmities, that the power of Christ may rest
upon me. (2 Cor. 12:7–9).*

Paul prayed three times for God to remove his thorn of flesh, but it wasn't God's plan to do so. Instead, He gave Paul abundant grace. God's grace is not just amazing—it's enough. His grace is so complete that the burdens of our pains, although they may still be there, can lessen greatly. Even to the point where they don't feel like burdens at all. His grace will work for any kind of condition, no matter how long the pain exists. God gives us grace for every situation.

Stay on the Potter's Wheel

In order to be successful in life and to overcome struggles, we must have staying power when suffering comes. This means we have to stay with God and trust Him. It takes courage to stay in the fight, especially when it looks like we are losing. But in order for lasting change to take place, we have to allow God to mold us and to make us over again.

Many people do not understand the process of the potter's wheel. The potter's wheel is not to punish us, but to shape us into the masterpiece which God has designed for us. God knows exactly what we are to become. Our lives have already been mapped out. It's up to us to strive for obedience to His will and to stay on the potter's wheel in the hands of the potter.

When young, I mixed dirt with water to make mud pies. I also took mounds of clay and molded it into different shapes and images. While dirt and clay yielded to my molding, I have not always been still while God crafted me into something useful. When things got tough, although I wanted to leap off, I had to stay on the wheel and allow God to fix my broken places and remove the afflictions, trauma, and all the misfortunes from my past. Uncomfortable at best, God removed my bruises and healed my scars.

Scripture reassured me it was for my benefit and necessary to bring me into fulfillment of God's plan. I had to give in, stop fighting, and allow His hands to work in my life. Though not easy, I trusted God when the shaping process seemed difficult to bear.

> *"But now, O LORD, thou art our father; we are the clay, and thou our potter; and we all are the work of thy hand" (Isa. 64:8).*

Sometimes, we know the thing we need most is for God to work us like clay. Instead of surrendering, however, we run the other way for fear of the pain. But only the Lord can restore us with a gentle hand when we are broken. Besides, running from our problems only increases the distance to the solution.

I pray the Lord will help you see His hand at work in every situation, as well as stay committed to the molding process, knowing something beautiful will emerge.

The Refiner's Fire

Metals are placed in the fire to remove unwanted materials and to enhance their qualities. When we endure suffering, we go into a refiner's fire which God uses to purify our hearts from the inside out. He desires to remove those things of no value to us. Also, He seeks to enhance us and desires nothing but excellence. By burning away the imperfections and impurities, God develops our characters and set us up for the biggest blessing we could ever imagine. We can read Christian books, obtain advice from godly leaders, sit in church on Sundays, attend Bible class during the week, and still not become purified. Busyness will not purify us. We must be placed in the refiner's fire.

Life in the refiner's fire requires trust in the unchanging purified love of God. As the heat of my painful circumstances intensified, I knew God walked beside me, whatever suffering I endured. For the furnace of affliction melted away those insignificant things holding me back and made my faith bright, intact, and strong.

I now realize God used this process to draw me closer to Him. Although painful, I know the testing was necessary, and I had to endure it in order to become the person God intends for me to be.

In the Bible, Job lost his family, health, finances, and friends. He went through the fire and reigned over suffering because he trusted God.

> *"But he knoweth the way that I take: when he hath tried me, I shall come forth as gold" (Job 23:10).*

Job suffered much, but he was determined to come out on top just like gold. When mined from the earth, gold looks nothing like a shiny necklace or twenty-four-carat gold rings. Instead, it looks dark and dull since it is usually mixed with rocks. When the heat removes the rocks, the gold comes forth. The hotter the fire, the purer the gold. Gold is tested by fire, but we are tested by pain and suffering. We may not know what troubles come our way, but we do know whose hands we are in. And when God has tried us in the fire, we will come out shining brighter than ever.

Wrestling with God

Oftentimes, we think the enemy plots our suffering. We see him as the one who fights us and slow us down, when really it is the Lord's doing. God challenges us to come up higher and to go deeper in Him. It's the Lord Himself trying to do a good work in us.

In a wrestling match, you grab each other and try to pin one another down. When we are pinned down by God, He means business. But we have to contend with Him if we want a breakthrough in our lives. We have to confront our weaknesses, failures, sins, and all the things hurting us and face God.

During my seasons of struggle, I sought God and wondered why things were so tough for me. The Lord spoke to me through another individual who told me I was wrestling with God. I didn't realize I wrestled, but I sure felt tired. After pleading with God night and day and spending hours crying out to Him, I felt exhausted. I just wanted to move far away. During those times, I wondered why He didn't seem to be with me. Later I realized God didn't need to be with me. I needed to be with Him. I waited on God to bless me and my plans, but God said no. I had to get with Him in order to receive His blessings.

Jacob is one of my favorite biblical characters. Why? Because I have always felt if God would bless Jacob, a person who was basically a thief, deceitful, and manipulating, then surely, I had a chance. Genesis 32 gives an interesting account of Jacob's life. While Jacob was all alone one night, God came out of nowhere and sought him out for a wrestling match.

> *And Jacob was left alone; and there wrestled a man with him until the breaking of the day. And when he saw that he prevailed not against him, he touched the hollow of his thigh; and the hollow of Jacob's thigh was out of joint, as he wrestled with him. And he said, let me go, for the day breaketh. And he said, I will not let thee go, except thou bless me. And he said unto him, what is thy name? And he said, Jacob. And he said, thy name shall be called no more Jacob, but Israel: for as a prince hast thou power with God and with men, and hast prevailed. (Gen. 32:24–28).*

Jacob left the wrestling match a different person. He had a limp, but God also gave him a new name, Israel. Jacob's name was changed to Israel because he wrestled with God and was now a changed man. When God changes our names, it's a blessing and means He has changed His description of us. When wrestling with God, we have to remain in the ring, even if on the ropes. We can't afford to leave empty-handed. When we wrestle with God and don't let go, He will change our names, our circumstances, and courses of life.

Die Already

God has not promised us an easy way or a road of convenience. He should know since His son walked it before us. With each step He took for us, carrying the cross, He realized this walk required submitting to the Father's will. Just as we have suffered, Jesus suffered in the garden of Gethsemane and was tortured during His crucifixion.

> *"Saying, Father, if thou be willing, remove this cup from me: nevertheless, not my will, but thine, be done" (Luke 22:42).*

I have often pleaded with God to remove my cup of suffering. Ready for the madness to be over, I wanted to get on with life. But God wasn't calling me to a crown, He was calling me to a cross. Besides, if I backed out, I would never see the point of all the pain. All I could take from my struggles were the humiliation and pressure I faced. I didn't want to keep prevailing in the garden of Gethsemane. How could I get through my cross quicker? I looked at Jesus and how He endured suffering. There I found my answer . . . the secret passage of getting through the cross is to die.

> *"Then came the soldiers, and brake the legs of the first, and of the other which was crucified with him. But when they came to Jesus, and saw that he was dead already, they brake not his legs" (John 19:32–33).*

Jesus knew how to die. He didn't even have to get His legs broken. In the same way, we don't have to face the same pressure repeatedly before we surrender. We just need to die to ourselves and surrender to His will. The Lord has a plan for us and has orchestrated all the events in our lives. He has worked through situations and relationships, moving all the right people into place. At just the right time, He applies the right amount of pressure needed to change us and make us better suited for His kingdom.

It took me a while to catch on to how God worked. Once enlightened, I submitted and "died already," like Jesus.

A Vessel of Honor

God wants to bring us out of bondage and make us vessels of honor. For it is not His will for us to perish. God wants to make us into something which will bring Him pleasure. He desires for us to become His choicest of oil and new wine. And God knows His best oils and wines are pressed and squeezed by the weights of circumstances and situations.

I made some terrible mistakes and did some things which controlled my life. I felt as though I had done irreversible damage and God could never use me.

But God never throws away a piece of His clay. When I make bad mistakes, the potter can't do anything else but to crush me and break me down. He has to remold me and reshape me into a beautiful vessel which will bring honor to Him. God is in the renewing and reshaping business. He can change us in just one instant, if only we will allow Him to do so.

> But in a great house there are not only vessels of gold and of silver, but also of wood and of earth; and some to honour, and some to dishonor. If a man therefore purge himself from these, he shall be a vessel unto honour, sanctified, and meet for the master's use, and prepared unto every good work. (2 Tim. 2:20–21).

God takes pride in polishing us into vessels of honor. People will look at our lives, the broken places from where we came and the breakthroughs we've had and declare, "It was nobody but God." Once God cuts away the knots, strongholds, and bad habits, we become usable vessels in the master's hands. I could only be where I am today because of God's fashioning hand.

Broken to Be a Blessing

One of God's goals in allowing us to suffer is to get our focus off ourselves and to respond to others' needs. Through our suffering, He wants to broaden our views and mold us to be like Him.

Then after suffering, I encourage you to be a blessing by ministering comfort to others who suffer. You will be able to truly say, "I know how you feel. I have been in your shoes." Feeling alone is a difficult part of suffering. It can feel like you are all alone in your pain and no one cares. The comfort of someone who has known the same pain is priceless. It feels as if you're sitting by a warm fireplace sipping on hot chocolate.

In order for me to minister to others, I first had to walk through the valley of distress. My pain gave me a tender heart toward others in pain. I wanted to bless someone else with comfort and hope. Someone else needed what I could give them because of what I had gone through.

When God allowed Joseph to suffer, He didn't just bless Joseph in the long run. He blessed Joseph's family and the nations.

> *"But as for you, ye thought evil against me; but God meant it unto good, to bring to pass, as it is this day, to save much people alive" (Gen. 50:20).*

Suffering blesses others by developing compassion and mercy in us. We can comfort others with the same comfort we have received from God, because we have experienced the reality of the Holy Spirit being there for us, walking with us in our pain. Therefore, we can turn around and bless others in their pain, showing the compassion our own sufferings have produced in us.

20

Pain: Part of the Plan

God has a plan for each of us. Before we were created, God skillfully crafted all our days. He nestled dreams and visions deep within our souls before He created time. God alone knows the story from beginning to end.

Oftentimes we know God has a plan for us, but we don't always like the plan because it comes with pain and troubles. We struggle to understand God's master plan and can't comprehend God's work because His ways are so much higher than our ways. Although we may not always understand this painful plan, we can still trust Him. For God always knows what He is doing, even when we don't. He never makes mistakes.

God knows because He is the architect and has the blueprint. He has already designed our lives, down to every little detail.

My life has been one big story. God has placed some difficult chapters in my story book which have been hard for me to get through. Oftentimes I wanted to quit. I experienced pain, sorrow, sadness, and suffering. At times, I cried myself to sleep at night. But I had to remember God knows best and to rely on Him during those trying times. When I was baffled by all the twists and turns, God still sustained me and ensured I made it through.

The same God who created me loves me, and He loves you too. His love comes with many promises for His children, including hope and potential.

> *"For I know the thoughts that I think toward you, saith the LORD, thoughts of peace, and not of evil, to give you an expected end" (Jer. 29:11).*

Our futures are not determined by our own actions or by the forces of our circumstances, however great they may seem. Our futures are determined by the plans God has for us. Even when we hit those painful chapters, we can take God at His Word. Scripture confirms He will keep His promises.

I could not quit on God because He did not quit me. Even when the road got tough, I had to keep traveling. God has a plan for my life, and He has one for you too.

Questioning God

During some of my darkest days I sought answers from the Lord. Lord, why so much heartache, and so much pain? Why do I keep going through the same things over and over? Why all this drama in my life? Why must I keep going after people who hurt me? I sought wisdom by asking God for direction. But is it okay to question God?

I have always been told if you don't know something, ask. I went to God with some difficult questions about my life and sought to find the answers. I just wanted to find out the "why" behind it all. I figured if I knew why, I could probably deal with it better. I would never accuse God of any wrongdoings. For such an attitude would be wrong. I went to God with respect and honor, realizing He is perfect in wisdom and knows all things. There is nothing sinful about questioning God. I found Scripture where even Jesus questioned God.

> *"Now from the sixth hour there was darkness over all the land unto the ninth hour. And about the ninth hour Jesus cried with a loud voice, saying, Eli, Eli, lama sabachthani? That is to say, my God, my God, why hast thou forsaken me?" (Matt. 27:45–46).*

Jesus came to earth to die for our sins. He even knew the appointed time. But Jesus still felt alone when it happened because it seemed God had left Him. Jesus wanted to know God was still with Him. Jesus's loud cry reflected the emotional pain He felt by being alone, as well as the excruciating physical pain on the cross. Jesus never got an answer from God on that day. So the issue is not whether we should question God, the issue is for what manner and for what reason we question Him.

I didn't have to die for anyone. But I was curious and wanted to know what was going on. It appeared I was left to fend for myself. I questioned God in faith and was willing to be content with His answer or even if He never answered at all. I have heard some people say Christians are not supposed to question God. But this is not what the Bible says.

> *"If any of you lack wisdom, let him ask of God, that giveth to all men liberally, and upbraideth not; and it shall be given him" (James 1:5).*

Our questions do not intimidate God. Instead, He invites us to approach Him. He says if we need wisdom, inquire of Him. He wants us to come to Him when we are confused and desire to know the purpose behind all the drama and chaos in our lives. So that's exactly what I did. I wasn't questioning God's goodness or His character, I questioned why certain things happened in my life. Although God may not answer our questions in the way we want, He welcomes sincere questions from our hearts.

A Divine Comeback

Nothing in life is happenstance, although our free will exists. With God, no accidents or coincidences occur, as everything has His seal of approval for our growth and change. As spiritual beings having human experiences, we may feel we've been thrust into unreasonable situations. We feel we have been set back by unexpected turns for the worse. Often, family setbacks or the loss of a loved one make us wonder if God is with us and if we will ever recover.

There have been many times in my life I didn't know why my plans got derailed. At first glance, it seemed all was lost. Instead of keeping an attitude of expectancy, I got caught up in the situation. When things looked bad, I felt bad. I worried and feared things would not be rectified. I fed into the enemy's lies and adopted a pessimistic outlook. I felt I must have done something awful bad to be going through what I experienced. But pain and suffering are not always connected to sin. Some things happened in my life which made no sense to me. I didn't do anything to cause the situation. It just came about on its own.

When things happen unexpectedly, God can use it to show His mighty work. It's just a divine setup for something awesome to happen in our lives. Our setbacks are just setups for comebacks. In the Bible, God showed up unexpectedly in the life of a man who was born blind.

> "And as Jesus passed by, he saw a man which was blind from his birth. And his disciples asked him, saying, Master, who did sin, this man, or his parents, that he was born blind?" (John 9:1–2).

The disciples asked Jesus if the man was born blind because of his own sins or the sins of his parents. They wanted to connect his blindness and suffering to sin. But Jesus said this was not the case. Sins of the past do not always correlate with specific suffering in the present. Instead of looking for the cause, Jesus pointed them to the purpose. Sin didn't cause his blindness. It was so the works of God might be displayed in him. The blind man had suffered a setback. He endured a serious handicap which caused major challenges for him. He had to go through life without being able to see the beautiful flowers, pretty, blue sky, and even his own parents. He likely felt rejected, ashamed, and unloved most of his life. Yet, all along, Jesus had a plan to display His miraculous healing power through the man's restored vision.

Though not easy to understand, God sometimes allows pain, struggles, and trials to be part of our lives. While He allows it, He also uses it to grow us spiritually if we will trust Him enough to go through it.

When suffering a setback, it's time to rejoice, not lose heart! Why? Because God is getting ready to give you a far greater blessing than you ever expected. Your setback is not God setting you aside. He will far exceed your expectations.

Remember, your setback is God's setup for your comeback!

Obedience Brings Healing

God has been so good to me. He has healed my broken heart and delivered me from pain, shame, and hurts. One day during my quiet time with the Lord, I expressed gratitude for all His grace and mercy shown toward me over the years. I said, "Lord, how can I ever thank you for all you have done for me?" In that moment, I heard something deep down in my spirit say, "Put it in a book." I thought my hearing must have been off because the Lord knew I had never written a book. I just like to read what others have written. I continued to sit in the Lord's presence as if I expected Him to tell me something different. After all, the idea of penning a book had never crossed my mind. Plus, I didn't think I had the skills to put it all together or the patience to see it through to completion.

Shortly after this encounter, He spoke to me again in a dream, which confirmed I had heard Him clearly the first time. I would like to tell you I jumped up immediately and started working on the book, but the truth is I placed it in the back of my mind and even forgot it for a season. When God tells us to do something, there's a reason behind it. He is not interested in us just doing something for nothing. I had a choice to make. I could stay in my comfort zone or choose God. God will require you to use your faith if you want to be healed, just like the blind man had to come out of his place of comfort in order to receive his sight.

> *When he had thus spoken, he spat on the ground, and made clay of the spittle, and he anointed the eyes of the blind man with the clay, And said unto him, Go, wash in the pool of Siloam, (which is by interpretation, Sent.) He went his way therefore, and washed, and came seeing. (John 9:6–7).*

The blind man's sight was restored, but it came after he obeyed and went to wash in the pool of Siloam. He did not question Jesus, saying why do I have to go? Or why did you put that mud on my eyes? He just obeyed God and went. As a result of obedience, he received his healing.

Unlike the blind man, initially I refused to move on what God told me to do. Instead of obeying, I did a lot of questioning, running, and filling my life with other unimportant stuff. I wanted to know how I was going to get started and thought I needed all the details up front. But God did not disclose them.

When God speaks to us, we have to trust and obey Him even if we do not have all the information. God will give us more knowledge as we need it and when we are ready to handle it.

We don't always choose correctly or move swiftly, but God is gracious enough to take all our missteps and fit them into His master plan. Don't allow a disobedient past to prohibit you from having an appointed future. It's only on the path of obedience we come to receive our healing and to know our purposes, not when we're drifting off on our own.

Pain Is a Piece of the Puzzle

Pain is a part of life. We have all gone through things we didn't understand.

I once enjoyed putting puzzles together. I loved looking at the pictures on the front of the boxes showing what the puzzles were supposed to look like. Oftentimes, I'd pick out ocean scenes. As a whole, the puzzles reflected beauty. But when I took pieces out of the boxes and looked at them individually, sometimes they looked strange, like they wouldn't fit anywhere. When I'd finally get all the pieces put together, those "strange-looking" pieces fit right in, and I'd have works of art.

In the same manner, sometimes we look at pieces in our lives that don't seem to fit. When we go through a divorce, our business goes bankrupt, or we or a loved one are diagnosed with a terminal illness, we deny it could be a part of God's plan. But even through painful times, we have to trust God when the puzzle piece doesn't make sense. God doesn't make mistakes. He's already planned your life and laid out all the pieces.

> *"For I know the plans I have for you," says the* LORD. *"They are plans for good and not for disaster, to give you a future and a hope" (Jer. 29:11, NLT).*

I mention this Scripture in a previous section, but it's so convincing that it's worth repeating because God's plans are really for good, and they give us hope and a future. So that piece of your life that's painful and doesn't look like it fits anywhere will fit perfectly when everything comes together. Just like God planned it.

My Life Will Never Be the Same

It is not the pain we need to focus on. It's what we do in our times of pain which is the most important. Pain changed me. Through heartaches, losses, and disappointments, I have gotten through them all by the grace of God. But I am a different person now. I have decided to come out better, not bitter. I could have come out with a chip on my shoulder, blaming God and others. Instead, I decided to come out stronger, with a greater confidence in God.

I now have a new passion, and I am excited about the opportunities which lie ahead for me. My challenge to you today is to not just go through it but grow through it. Don't just survive but thrive. It will make you wiser, develop your character, and will give you the confidence and knowledge to lean on God through tough times.

The pain is not there to stop us, rather to prepare, increase, and develop us. God knows what He has placed on the inside of us. He knows how much pain and adversity we can handle. If the things we went through could destroy us, God would not have allowed them to happen. For He has ordered all our steps.

"The steps of a good man are ordered by the LORD:
and he delighteth in his way" (Ps. 37:23).

The enemy may turn on the fire in the furnace, but God controls the temperature. He will not allow you to melt and be defeated. You must believe you can handle it. If you approach it with that attitude, you will come out better than before, and your life will never be the same.

Turn Your Pain into Purpose

Your pain wasn't for nothing, so don't waste it. I don't believe God allowed me to go through all of that just for the heck of it. There has got to be a reason I survived all that drama. There's got to be something ahead of me which is far greater than what stands behind me.

Don't get embarrassed by your past. If you try to hide it and hold it back, it doesn't do anybody any good. But if you are honest with God and yourself, as well as transparent with other people, God can use the very thing that hurt you the most. He can even use the very thing you are most disappointed in about yourself and you wish had never happened. God can use your pain for your benefit and for

His purpose if you are willing to share your brokenness. He can use it to help others. So don't just keep it to yourself.

> *"He comforts us in all our troubles so that we can comfort others. When they are troubled, we will be able to give them the same comfort God has given us"* (2 Cor. 1:4, NLT).

Your greatest ministry can be birthed out of your pain and difficult experiences. God allowed it because He can trust you. He knows He can count on you to take the same love, healing, and encouragement, and share it with others. Who can be more sympathetic and compassionate than someone who has already been through what another person is going through? Who can help somebody going through a terrible illness better, other than someone who has gone through it before? And who can better help someone who's been hurt by a painful past than someone God has healed and delivered from a painful past? If you stay in faith and stay the course, God will turn your pain into purpose and will give you a new talent, new ministry, new friendships, and take you to a new level.

There's Purpose behind Our Problems

God often allows problems to push us into our purposes and destinies. Without troubles, many of us would never fulfill the purpose for which God created us. Sometimes an assault invades our lives, creating pain so deep all we know to do is press into God with everything we have. When we discover purpose, we will feel God's love despite the problems.

When I first started experiencing problems in life, I tried to alleviate them. But after a season of extreme emotional pressures, I moved to a new and deeper relationship with God. I began to discover things about myself and about God which I never would have discovered without being motivated by problems and stress. Gradually, my heart moved from my issues. I no longer sought

God for deliverance from my troubles, I sought Him because He is God. When my heart moved from trying to solve all my problems, I found myself moving into a new destiny and calling for my life. God separated me from my old life in the process. All the hardships of my past prepared me for what God has called me to do.

> *"And we know that all things work together for good to them that love God, to them who are the called according to his purpose" (Rom. 8:28).*

Through all the trauma and pain, I have learned to not ignore those painful events. Instead, I have allowed God to use them to shift me to healing and breakthrough.

Today, allow God to move you from all the problems in your life to a place of purpose. Allow God to show you the secret things He has reserved for you as a result of the troubles and the crises you have gone through.

God Chooses Imperfect People

A common misconception is God chooses people who are highly qualified to further His kingdom. But this concept has proven not to be true. Throughout Scripture, we see God using imperfect, flawed people who didn't have their lives together. He didn't call the popular, wealthy, or successful to carry the Gospel, but He used the broken, poor, and confused.

I felt I had done too much wrong and experienced too much damage to be any good for God. I had come a long way, but I still had some distance to go. I kept waiting for God to perfect all of my flaws. But He didn't. I still have some. Despite this, I had to go on and serve the Lord. I had to stop waiting for when I finally had it all together. God calls imperfect people, which means we all qualify. It doesn't matter where people come from, what they did or who they used to be. Jesus uses lost people for His kingdom. Still not convinced? The Bible has many examples of God's imperfect heroes.

Abraham lied about Sarah.

> *"And Abraham said of Sarah his wife, she is my sister: and Abimelech, king of Gerar, sent and took Sarah" (Gen. 20:2).*

Peter denied Christ three times.

> *"But he began to curse and to swear, saying, I know not this man of whom ye speak. And the second time the cock crew. And Peter called to mind the word that Jesus said unto him, before the cock crow twice, thou shalt deny me thrice. And when he thought thereon, he wept" (Mark 14:71–72).*

Noah was a drunk.

> *"And Noah began to be a husbandman, and he planted a vineyard: And he drank of the wine and was drunken; and he was uncovered within his tent" (Gen. 9:20, 21).*

If you think you are not good enough to be used by God, just remember Jesus used a bunch of imperfect people to share hope to a flawed world. In Him, we find acceptance. Jesus didn't call the equipped, instead He equips the called. Regardless of your story, God can use you. He actually prefers people who know their weaknesses, see their flaws, admit their mistakes, and cry out to Him for help. He uses people who have fallen short in many ways and does some amazing things through them.

Birth Pains

God has placed purpose down on the inside of every person. The problem is nobody seems to want to go through the pain and the process of delivery. We are all called for greatness. But even greatness has to be birthed. When we are pregnant with purpose, there will become a season when it's time to deliver the thing God has placed inside of us. We are actually carrying something bigger than what we could ever imagine. God wants us to deliver His purpose throughout the earth, and He has given us the grace to endure. We can't try to get someone else to deliver for us. We each have our own purposes, and we have to birth our own babies.

When the delivery of what God has placed in us is at hand, the birth pains begin. The pains come and go until they come faster and closer together. For me, the birthing process started to get very painful as certain situations, people, and things began to move out of my life. Some people began to make life more difficult for me.

But we can't get distracted by birth pains. It's all part of the spiritual birthing process. Travailing in prayer gave me the strength I needed to go all the way. Travailing in prayer will enable me to continue pushing God's promises through to fruition. I know you must be tired and uncomfortable as the pressure and intensity mounts and your season is getting closer. Most likely you feel you can't make it through delivery, but you have to make it. There are people waiting on what you are carrying, plus God will not allow you to give up.

> *"Being confident of this very thing, that he which hath begun a good work in you will perform it until the day of Jesus Christ" (Phil. 1:6).*

If God has given you a purpose to carry, start getting excited! Because whatever God has started in your life, He will finish. You may be at the point of your greatest deliverance and think you will not be able to make it, but you can. You are going to give birth. The pain and pressure all come with the delivery. But when the baby is born, you will see that all the cries and pain were a part of the plan. It was all worth it. When you receive the abundant blessings of God, the pain pales in comparison.

God's Plan Will Come to Pass

Oftentimes we think because we have made mistakes and are not where we want to be in life, we must have stopped God's plan. We are not powerful enough to stop God's plans. There is nothing we have done which has been a surprise to God. He already knew we would mess up, and He already has the mercy we need to shake off the guilt and keep it moving.

The enemy does not desire our past. He wants our future. He knows God has something amazing for us. While he may know about it, he can't do anything about it. We don't have to force things to happen. All we must do is seek God and stay close to Him, and we will come into His purpose. We are not here by mistake. God has a specific plan for our lives. We haven't made too many mistakes or missed too many opportunities. God directs our steps and has it all lined up, every detail.

When I sang in the church choir, we sang a song called "God Said It and That Settles It." God has the final say. He makes a way, even when we don't see a way. Where I was born or how I was reared doesn't have to stop God's purpose for me. Before anyone put a curse on me, God put a blessing on me, and the blessing overrides the curse every time. It doesn't matter what people have said about me, it only matters what God said.

> *"For the LORD of hosts hath purposed, and who shall disannul it? And his hand is stretched out, and who shall turn it back?" (Isa. 14:27).*

Everything God has planned for us will come to pass. For no one has the power to defeat His purposes. Although life may hit us with disasters, tragedies and blows, it has no power to hinder the plans of God. None can disarm them. The pains we have endured will serve as a launching pad to propel us into our life's purpose. When we follow God's blueprint, our lives will take shape, exactly like He intended.

For God's plan will come to pass. It won't hurt anymore!

About the Author

A native Mississippian, Dr. Arvis Murrell is passionate about providing encouragement, strength, and comfort to shattered lives. She understands life's struggles and loves to share her story of how God transformed her from brokenness to a life of wholeness.

She has served people in the mid-South for more than twenty-five years as a registered nurse displaying empathy and compassion. Her most recent nursing experience involves caring for those with cancer and other life-threatening diseases. Arvis is also a Christian counselor who has helped thousands heal emotionally, particularly when dealing with death and divorce.

As a child, Arvis loved to read, sing, and play outdoors. She is married to Carl Murrell, Sr. and they live in Cordova, Tennessee. Together they enjoyed traveling and spending time with their blended family of six children.

To contact Arvis, please email at arvis.murrell@yahoo.com.